How to Choose your GCSEs

Essential Information about
Key Stage 4
Courses and Examinations

Alan Vincent

TROTMAN

This fifth edition published in 1995 in Great Britain by
Trotman & Company Ltd,
12 Hill Rise, Richmond, Surrey TW10 6UA
© Trotman and Company Limited
British Library Cataloguing in Publication Data
A catalogue record for this book is available from
the British Library
ISBN 0 85660 203 5
Printed and bound in Great Britain
Redwood Books, Trowbridge, Wiltshire

YOUR GRANT MAY BE FROZEN,

BUT OUR OVERDRAFT ISN'T.

Surviving on a grant alone may be worthy of some qualification.

That's why Midland offers an interest-free overdraft that rises from £500 for the first year, to £600 for the second and £700 for the third.

And, unlike some other overdraft facilities, it remains interest-free the whole time you're at college.

Free banking goes without saying, regardless of whether or not your account is in credit. On the odd occasion that it is, a handsome interest rate is paid on the balance.

The Autocheque card, with Switch facility, gives instant access to money 24 hours a day, 7 days a week, via the country's largest network of cash machines.

If you think you can handle credit, there's the option to apply for a fee-free Access and Visa card.

FOR FURTHER DETAILS CONTACT YOUR LOCAL MIDLAND BRANCH OR TELEPHONE 0345 180180

In the branch is the student advisor, who can both answer questions and explain further all the services available.

So, if you're interested in opening an account drop into your local branch, and see if Midland can help thaw you out.

MIDLAND
The Listening Bank

Member HSBC Group

ABOUT THE AUTHOR

Alan Vincent graduated with a French degree from Reading University in 1964. After training as a teacher, he went to Nigeria to introduce French into a mixed boarding school and, as House Master, developed an interest in pastoral work. His first involvement in careers teaching came in 1969 at a comprehensive school in Hertfordshire - two years later Alan became Head of the Careers department and introduced Careers into the timetable. He then moved on to the North Oxfordshire Centre of Advanced Studies as Head of Guidance and Admissions, which led to his appointment as TVEI Co-ordinator for North Oxfordshire in September 1988.

Alan joined the Executive Council of the National Association of Careers & Guidance Teachers (NACGT) in 1976 and has been a Council member ever since. He was General Secretary from 1979 to 1984 and President from 1985 to 1987. Throughout his career he has made significant contributions to the development of careers education and guidance through his involvement in training courses run by NACGT, ICG, CRAC, NAPCE , LEA's and TECs. He presently works as self-employed consultant and current contracts include the co-ordination of a local Learning Partnership (a post-TVEI consortium of schools and colleges) and the management of an Education Business Partnership.

CONTENTS

**LOGIC WILL GET YOU FROM A TO B
BUT WITH IMAGINATION
YOU CAN CIRCLE THE WORLD.**

ENGINEERING & SYSTEMS SPONSORSHIPS

Einstein was no fool, and when he said these words he meant it!

The principle he expressed then is equally valid now.

And nowhere could this be more appropriate than at Ford today. With a pioneering history that brought motor transport within the reach of so many people, and a sales network that now circles the globe, it is impossible to overestimate the impact that Ford has had on the world.

Our continued success depends on many factors – not least of which is an intelligent, reasoned and logical approach to business. But it takes more than logic alone to make real progress and that is one of the reasons why we can offer such a unique and stimulating challenge to school leavers. In the motor industry, we are facing a time of greater change than ever before, and to meet these demands we rely on fresh ideas – from people with imagination.

Sponsorship is available to school leavers who plan to read either an engineering or a Systems/Information Technology degree at one of a number of approved higher education institutions. Students already at college should apply for our vacation training opportunities through their academic tutor.

For an information pack please write to Paul Mills, College Recruitment & Education Liaison, 1/360, Ford Motor Company Limited, Eagle Way, Brentwood, Essex CM13 3BW.
Tel: 01277 252328.

These vacancies are open to both men and women regardless of ethnic origin in line with Ford's equal opportunities policy.

1.GETTING THE FACTS STRAIGHT

The GCSE countdown for you has now begun. But what are you letting yourself in for? Let's begin by getting a few of the basic facts straight.

WHAT IS THE GCSE?

GCSE stands for the General Certificate of Secondary Education. It replaced GCE O-levels and CSEs.

WHO IS THE GCSE FOR?

YOU. It is designed as a two-year course of study for students in Years 10 and 11 (Years 11 and 12 in Northern Ireland).

At Key Stage 4 (KS4) GCSE is the main means of assessing attainment. At present we are in an interim period for the introduction of the National Curriculum in its revised form and for the drawing together of the National Curriculum and the criteria for the GCSE examinations. For courses beginning in September 1996, new GCSE courses will be introduced which will fully reflect the revised National Curriculum.

CAN EVERYBODY TAKE THE GCSE?

Yes. The GCSE is open to anyone who can meet its requirements, regardless of their age or circumstances of study. The GCSE is therefore available to both mature and private candidates as well as all those in schools and colleges.

WHEN DO I TAKE THE EXAM?

The usual age to sit the end-of-course exam is 16...but there are no hard and fast rules. You can take it before or after that age.

There is some more information about taking the GCSE early and its implications in the next chapter, about GCSE and the National Curriculum.

WHEN CAN I SIT THE EXAM?

There are two sittings each year. Most people will take the exam in the Summer when all subjects are on offer. In most subjects, the exams are held in May/June.

The second, or Winter sitting is in either November or January, depending on what course you are taking. Not all subjects are offered in the Winter examinations.

WHY DO I NEED TO TAKE THE GCSE?

Sixteen is a turning point in every young person's life. It is a time of change. Some of you may leave school and take a job or start on a training placement. Most of you will stay on in full-time education, at either school or college, for at least one or two more years, in order to improve your range of skills and qualifications. For some the aim will be to take further examinations, like A-levels or a General National Vocational Qualification (GNVQ), and perhaps go on to university or a college of higher education.

For all, GCSE offers an opportunity to assess your skills and abilities and help you decide how these may be sharpened and directed along more specific lines.

WHAT MAKES THE GCSE DIFFERENT FROM EXAMINATIONS IN THE PAST

GCSE is designed to relate to students' everyday lives. For example, syllabuses address economic, political, social and environmental matters, where these are appropriate and relevant to the particular subject. They are also expected to provide opportunities for the appropriate use of Information Technology, to complement and reinforce work done in that particular subject.

With the GCSE, there is more emphasis on problem solving and using the knowledge you have gained. That is why GCSE courses include practical work, oral work, fieldwork, investigations, projects, even group work. The result is courses that are more interesting, more inventive and more useful. It all means less time being a passive learner and more time spent on projects, problem solving and finding out for yourself.

Most GCSEs include coursework – that's work that you do during the two years. And the marks for your coursework count towards your final result. Exams are fine for testing knowledge and, to some extent, understanding. But they favour people with a good memory and there are many skills which an exam can't test at all. How, for example, can an exam show how good you are at looking up information and using it? Or at carrying out your own project? The GCSE format will not only test your knowledge of formulae for scientific experiments, but also how well you apply them in the lab – after all, what use is it being able to remember something you don't understand and are not able to use?

This is where the GCSE scores – it is designed to test ALL your skills.

2. GCSE AND THE NATIONAL CURRICULUM

WHAT IS THE NATIONAL CURRICULUM?

The Education Reform Act of 1988 requires all schools in the maintained sector to provide a broad and balanced curriculum for students of compulsory school age. This is known as the National Curriculum.

WHAT SUBJECTS ARE INCLUDED IN THE NATIONAL CURRICULUM?

Basically, the National Curriculum consists of ten subjects – with Welsh as an additional subject for Welsh-speaking schools.

In Key Stages 1-3, the following subjects are included in the National Curriculum:

- English
- Mathematics
- Science
- Technology (Design & Technology and Information Technology are the separate components of Technology, but Information Technology, in many aspects, has now achieved separate subject status.)
- History
- Geography
- Art
- Music
- Physical Education
- A Modern Foreign Language (in Key Stage 3)

Religious Education must also be part of the curriculum for all students.

At Key Stage 4, the range of subjects that pupils may study and in which they may be tested is increased, but only the following subjects remain compulsory:

4

- English
- Mathematics
- Science
- Physical Education (from August 1995)
- Technology (from August 1996)
- A Modern Foreign Language.

In Wales, Welsh is added in relation to schools which are not Welsh-speaking.

Wales also has separate subject Orders from England in History, Geography, Art, Music and Welsh.

As with Physical Education, Religious Education, Sex Education and Careers Education must be part of the curriculum for all students, but there are no statutory examination requirements in any of these subjects.

WHAT IS THE EFFECT ON GCSE?

There are National Curriculum guidelines as to the knowledge, skills and understanding that all students are expected to have acquired in each subject by the ages of 7 (age 8 in Northern Ireland), 11, 14 and 16.

GCSE is at present the main means of assessing what students have achieved in each subject during KS4. The future role of the GNVQ in this context is not yet entirely clear, although it is likely to make a significant contribution for an increasing number of young people – either through the experience of specific units or through the new Part One GNVQ qualification. There is further information on the role of GNVQ in KS4 towards the end of this Chapter.

GCSE criteria have been going through a lengthy revision process. Syllabuses meeting National Curriculum criteria are already operating in English, Mathematics and Science, but the National Curriculum itself has been undergoing an extensive review. Revised National Curriculum Orders were published at the beginning of 1995.

5

The new Orders resulted in further revisions in GCSE criteria and the examination groups are now preparing new syllabuses, which are due to be sent to schools in January 1996, with a view to their being taught from September 1996.

The new criteria take account of the latest thinking on what knowledge, understanding and skills young people ought to be acquiring through their studies. Progression and continuity are also receiving greater emphasis, with the need, for example, to ensure the appropriate links between KS3 and KS4.

The following new GCSE syllabuses will be available for National Curriculum and related subjects for examination in 1998:

- Art
- Design & Technology (short and full courses)
- English
- English Literature
- Geography
- History
- Home Economics
- Information Technology
- Mathematics
- Modern Foreign Languages (short and full courses)
- Music
- Physical Education
- Science (single and double award)
- Science: Biology
- Science: Chemistry
- Science: Physics
- Welsh
- Welsh Literature
- Welsh Second Language

Some other subjects governed by subject-specific GCSE criteria already have new syllabuses. The first examinations in these subjects are scheduled for Summer 1996:

- Business Studies
- Classical Civilisation
- Economics
- Greek
- Latin
- Law
- Politics
- Psychology
- Religious Studies
- Science: Environmental
- Science: Geology
- Science: Rural
- Social Science
- Sociology

All remaining GCSE subjects will have new syllabuses available for examination in 1999.

In the case of National Curriculum subjects, all the new syllabuses are designed to cover the KS4 programmes of study.

WILL THIS MAKE A DIFFERENCE TO ME? WILL I HAVE NO CHOICE ABOUT TAKING THE NATIONAL CURRICULUM SUBJECTS?

The introduction of the National Curriculum takes some of the optional element out of the 14-16 stage.

For example, you may be taught either Double or Single Science at KS4. In some schools, the National Curriculum requirement is also met by pupils taking all three of the separate sciences of Biology, Chemistry and Physics.

The Government believes that Double Science or the three separate sciences should be taken by the great majority of pupils. The alternative Single Science course is intended for a minority of students who may need, for whatever reason, to spend more time on other subjects.

Single Science has been designed to be just as challenging at all levels, and will lead to a single award GCSE. One important point to note is that the student who takes the Single Science course and who then wishes to continue with study of A-level Science post-16 may need to take a bridging course before or at the start of the A-levels.

In Design & Technology the requirement for pupils entering KS4 in 1994 and 1995 to study Technology as part of the National Curriculum was lifted. This was done to allow time for a revised Technology Order to be introduced for that Key Stage in 1996. In practice, many schools are continuing to offer examination courses in the interim period at KS4, to enable pupils to build on their previous work in the subject. For pupils entering KS4 in September 1995, it will therefore depend on the individual school as to whether Technology is a compulsory subject or not. But Design & Technology will be compulsory for all pupils entering KS4 in September 1996.

The National Curriculum is not intended to be a strait-jacket and the review of the National Curriculum carried out by Sir Ron Dearing in 1994 has led to greater flexibility, especially in KS4, where it is proposed that the statutory curriculum should occupy about 60% of the time, leaving 40% available for other options.

In Wales, there will be even more time for schools to use as they choose – half the timetable as opposed to 60% in England – because there are no requirements for Modern Foreign Languages, Technology or Information Technology.

WHAT WILL THIS FLEXIBILITY MEAN FOR ME?

Firstly, there will be more choice of course in some subjects. These courses will require different amounts of time on the timetable and will lead to different qualifications.

Short courses, as an alternative to a full GCSE, will become available (from September 1996) in subjects like Design & Technology, Information Technology, Modern Foreign Languages, Religious Education and Welsh Second Language (building on the current short course syllabus in the subject). Such courses will have half the value of a full GCSE and take up half the teaching time – so they might, for example, be completed in one year rather than the usual two.

Remember that you will be allowed to drop one or more subjects at the end of Key Stage 3, if this seems a good option for you.

Also, you will be able, either individually or on a whole class basis, to take GCSE early and then to drop the subjects that have been taken.

Finally, the vocational examining bodies, such as BTEC, City & Guilds and RSA will be providing an alternative to GCSE. We include more information about alternatives to GCSE at the end of this chapter.

WHAT WILL BE THE EFFECTS OF MY TAKING ONE OR MORE GCSEs EARLY?

There are specific National Curriculum Regulations which apply to whole classes of students taking GCSE (or equivalent) qualifications early. Under these Regulations, students who take GCSE (or an equivalent qualification) in a National Curriculum subject: **at the same time as the majority of students in their class, and before the start of the second year of KS4** will thereafter be excepted from the National Curriculum requirements relating to that subject. This exception applies irrespective of the level attained by the student in the examination. However, it does **not** apply to a short course, when both a full course and a short course are specified for the particular National Curriculum subject.

WHAT HAPPENS IF I AM IN THE FIRST YEAR OF GCSE AS THE MEANS OF ASSESSING A NATIONAL CURRICULUM SUBJECT?

When the provisions of a National Curriculum subject first apply to Year 10, the new GCSE examinations will not be available for the summer of that year. This is referred to as the 'transition year' for that subject.

Students in a transition year, who are taking GCSE a year early, are excepted from the requirements of the National Curriculum in order to allow them to follow an existing GCSE syllabus. This exception will continue to apply even if the student fails to take the examination at the time intended.

WHAT ARE THE ALTERNATIVES TO GCSE?

The General National Vocational Qualification (GNVQ) has already become a popular alternative to A-level or GCSE study post-16 in school sixth forms and in colleges.

GNVQ courses are offered at Foundation, Intermediate and Advanced levels and provide a broadly-based vocational education. Students are expected to acquire the basic skills and a body of knowledge relevant to a particular vocational area, such as Art & Design, Business, Health & Social Care, Leisure & Tourism, or Manufacturing.

In addition to acquiring the basic skills and a body of knowledge relevant to one of the vocational areas, all students have to achieve a range of core skills. Evidence of achievement, at an appropriate level is required in three mandatory core skill units: Communication, Application of Number and Information Technology.

For more information about GNVQs and the vocational areas available, see Chapter 12 – Life After GCSEs.

BUT WHAT ABOUT KEY STAGE 4?

The GNVQ is now to become the basis for alternative vocational pathways at Key Stage 4. The aim will be to assist progression into a vocational route post-16 and provide a foundation for further education and/or training within the National Vocational Qualification (NVQ) framework.

There are three ways in which students might in future have some involvement with GNVQs at KS4. These will complement the National Curriculum – and remember that all students must take the GCSE or equivalent in Maths, English and Science – and will provide a more appropriate route for the target group.

Taking a full Intermediate or Foundation GNVQ at KS4 would mean that there would be no time for subjects outside the mandatory curriculum. This is unlikely to be an attractive alternative for many schools.

In some schools, students will be able to take specific vocational units of interest. Unit credits gained in this way can count towards a full GNVQ taken at a later stage.

Finally, over 100 schools are to be involved in a national pilot, starting in September 1995 and aimed at developing a new curriculum framework for students aged 14-16 (with more schools joining in from September 1996). This new model will enable students to combine GCSE (or a vocational qualification equivalent to GCSE) in the compulsory subjects with other National Curriculum subjects (which may or may not be examined at GCSE) and other subjects or courses which lead to vocational qualifications. The overall title for this framework is the Part One GNVQ. It is intended that the Part One structure should be available to all schools from September 1997.

HOW WILL THIS PART ONE GNVQ FIT WITH GCSE?

Part One has been designed to take 20% of the curriculum time in KS4 and to provide a recognised qualification which is clearly worthwhile in its own right. It will offer a coherent package of GNVQ units and will be available at both Intermediate and Foundation levels.

GNVQ Intermediate Part One will consist of three vocational units and three core skills units and is designed to be the equivalent of two GCSEs at grades D-G.

Three subject areas are to be piloted in the first instance –
Business, Health & Social Care, and Manufacturing.

The intention is to encourage a more integrated approach to the
curriculum across subject boundaries. For example, revision to the
National Curriculum Subject Orders has taken account of core
skill requirements as expressed in GNVQ. So GCSE English will
contribute to core skill Communication and GCSE Maths will
contribute to core skill Application of Number.

Essentially, the range of possible courses at Key Stage 4 is as
follows:

Subject	National Curriculum requirement
Mathematics	Full course
English	Full course
Science	Single Science, Double Science or three separate Sciences
Welsh	Full course
Welsh Second Language	Full or short course
Technology	Full or short course
Modern Foreign Language	Full or short course
History	Optional
Geography	in both
Physical Education	Compulsory
Art	Optional
Music	
Part One GNVQ	NC courses as above

In schools in Wales where Welsh is a core subject, students will
take Welsh to GCSE. In schools where Welsh is a non-core
foundation subject, students will study Welsh at KS4, but not
necessarily to GCSE. A short course is available in Welsh as a
second language.

3. HOW THE GCSE EXAM WORKS

There are six different examining groups which set the examinations:

The Midland Examining Group (MEG);
The Northern Examining Association Board (NEAB);
The Southern Examining Group (SEG);
The Northern Ireland Council for the Curriculum, Examinations and Assessment (CCEA);
The University of London Examinations & Assessment Council (ULEAC);
The Welsh Joint Education Committee (WJEC).

Your school will normally be free to select courses of study set by any of the examining groups. Most teachers look carefully at the full range of syllabuses to find the course that seems the most interesting and useful – the one they hope you will enjoy and do best in.

WITH SIX DIFFERENT GROUPS SETTING THE EXAMS IN THE SAME SUBJECTS DO STANDARDS VARY?

Government statements and reports from HMI have raised some concern about the consistency of standards. In particular, the Examining Groups are being encouraged to apply more objective criteria for awarding and to be more rigorous in approaches and procedures across the Groups.

GCSE general criteria from Schools Curriculum and Assessment Authority (SCAA) already provide overall guidance on subject titles, the nature of syllabuses, assessment procedures and the general conduct of examinations. These general criteria require each syllabus to promote a balance of knowledge, under-standing and skills, also that student achievement will be assessed in each syllabus by a combination of coursework and terminal examination appropriate to the subject concerned.

In England, Wales and Northern Ireland the Examining Groups together form the Joint Council for the GCSE. The Joint Council provides a forum for discussion and the exchange of information. It is responsible for co-ordinating the work of the individual Groups and helping to establish nationally consistent practices. The Examining Groups have, for example, collaborated over the preparation of GCSE syllabuses for the National Curriculum core subjects of English, Mathematics and Science. Each Group put forward proposals to the Joint Council. From these proposals a suite of syllabuses was agreed by the Joint Council for the GCSE. As a consequence, for each core subject there is a range of syllabuses catering for the full range of needs.

All these moves are intended to ensure that syllabuses have the highest possible degree of consistency. SCAA works closely with the Joint Council and the individual Examining Groups to maintain GCSE standards and to continue to improve the effectiveness and fairness of the system.

HOW IS THE GCSE GRADED?

Examiners decide the grade boundaries for the award of grades A, C and F. The remaining grades are then awarded on an arithmetical basis. For example, for a particular syllabus the grade A boundary might be set at 300 marks and the grade C boundary at 220 marks; the grade B boundary would then be set half-way, at 260 marks.

In Modern Foreign Languages, a distinctive awarding system is used. A range of points – usually 7 – is available for each of the four language skills. GCSE grades are awarded on the number of points achieved on the subject as a whole (for example, an A grade is awarded for candidates who achieve 24 or more of the 28 points that are usually available.

In order to help parents understand the level of attainment signified by the GCSE grade awarded, new 'attainment descriptions' will be offered that relate to grades A, C and F, and below G.

HOW DIFFICULT IS IT TO ACHIEVE THE A*?

There is no limit on the number of starred A grades that are awarded in any one subject. Results depend entirely on the quality of the candidates' work.

About 3% of GCSE candidates achieved the new grade in the summer 1994 examinations – compared with 12% achieving the normal A grade.

WHAT HAPPENS IF MY GCSE PERFORMANCE DOES NOT EARN A GRADE G OR ABOVE?

If that were to happen, the performance would be reported on the results slip as U (for 'unclassified').

HOW WILL THE MARKS FOR MY GCSE BE ARRIVED AT?

In most subjects, the marks are made up of two parts.

Firstly, coursework done in Years 10 and 11 (Years 11 and 12 in Northern Ireland) is assessed. Secondly, an examination is held at the end of the two years. This is explained more fully in the next chapter.

WILL I LOSE MARKS FOR BAD SPELLING?

SCAA has developed marking criteria for use in GCSE terminal examinations. They apply to all subjects where candidates are required to write in sentences (in English or Welsh). They do not apply to multiple choice or practical tests.

For each GCSE subject, 5% of the marks for each written paper will be allocated to spelling, punctuation and grammar according to the following performance criteria.

Threshold performance: Candidates spell, punctuate and use the rules of grammar with reasonable accuracy; they use a limited range of specialist terms appropriately.

Intermediate performance: Candidates spell, punctuate and use the rules of grammar with considerable accuracy; they use a good range of specialist terms with facility.

High performance: Candidates spell, punctuate and use the rules of grammar with almost faultless accuracy, using a range of grammatical constructions; they also use a wide range of specialist terms adeptly and with precision.

Candidates below the threshold performance level will receive no marks for spelling, punctuation and grammar.

Although these criteria apply equally to all subjects, the overall effect on the whole subject grade will clearly be greater in those subjects where there is a larger writing component.

The criteria for English and Welsh make additional requirements for linguistic accuracy to be assessed. Performance in spelling, punctuation and grammar are a factor in determining the candidate's overall grade.

Marks are allocated for spelling in GCSE written coursework on the same basis as for GCSE terminal examinations.

There are special arrangements to exempt dyslexic and other handicapped students from this requirement.

DOES THIS MEAN THAT DICTIONARIES CANNOT BE USED IN EXAMINATIONS?

Dictionaries and spelling aids are no longer allowed, except for certain vocationally-slanted examinations and for candidates who are permitted to use a bilingual dictionary (after the school has made a special representation to which the Examining Group has agreed).

DO EMPLOYERS UNDERSTAND WHAT GCSES ARE?

Every attempt is being made to acquaint employers with recent changes. But you might still find yourself faced with a bewildered employer or personnel officer. Don't worry...help is at hand. On the back of the examination certificate you will receive, there is an explanation of how the exam works.

4. COURSEWORK IN FOCUS

We've mentioned 'coursework' several times. Now it's time to look at it in more detail.

WHAT IS COURSEWORK?

Coursework is work which is integral to the course. That means that it is usually done in class and is closely supervised by teachers.

It can take various forms such as assignments in English, History, Religious Studies; field work in Geography; practical and project work in Art, Mathematics, Technology and Science; compositions in Music.

Throughout your two years of study for GCSEs your teacher will set specific topics for you to do. These topics will be marked by your teacher and those marks will go towards your final GCSE results.

WHY IS COURSEWORK NECESSARY?

As mentioned previously, there are many skills that can't be tested by the traditional written exam – practical and oral skills, for example. Coursework gives you the chance to demonstrate the many abilities you have and so makes the final mark you receive much fairer.

Teachers, supported by the Examination Groups, are responsible for ensuring that students are engaged in suitable coursework, which is normally an essential ingredient to meet the specific subject requirements of the National Curriculum. Various HMI and OFSTED reports on quality and standards in GCSE examinations have found that both teacher assessment and the guidance provided by the examining groups to support teacher assessment of coursework are generally of a high standard.

18

WHICH SKILLS AND ABILITIES ARE TESTED THROUGH COURSEWORK?

Your performance in coursework will show if you are able to...

- research, collect, compare and organise information

- work in a group

- make accurate records and use your powers of observation through laboratory and field work

- plan and organise a long piece of work

- use apparatus and machinery

- communicate – and that means to listen as well as to talk and discuss

- investigate, plan and design

These are exactly the vocationally-related skills which employers value.

Coursework also encourages students to work independently and assists in the preparation for higher level studies, such as A and A/S levels and GNVQ Advanced courses.

WHEN WILL I DO THE COURSEWORK?

In some subjects you will start coursework during the first term of Year 10 (Year 11 in Northern Ireland), while with other subjects coursework may not start until Year 11 (Year 12 in Northern Ireland). It will all depend on the syllabus.

YES, BUT *WHEN* WILL I ACTUALLY DO COURSE-WORK? WILL IT CUT INTO MY SPARE TIME?

Some of the work will be done in class, some will be done as homework. Though your teachers may say it shouldn't take you any longer than your normal homework, it's only fair to say, if you want to do well, it probably will take more time.

IS THERE COURSEWORK IN ALL SUBJECTS?

Most Modern Foreign Languages include an oral, but there isn't necessarily any other coursework.

WHAT PERCENTAGE OF MARKS ARE GIVEN FOR COURSEWORK?

There must always be an externally set terminal examination. In the case of modular syllabuses, the terminal examination must account for at least 50% of the marks.

The weighting for coursework in all other syllabuses is set out below:

Art	up to 60%
Design & Technology	at least 40% and up to 60%
English	up to 40%
English Literature	up to 30%
Geography	at least 20% and up to 25%
History	up to 25%
Home Economics	up to 50%
Information Technology	at least 40% and up to 60%
Mathematics	up to 20%
Modern Foreign Languages	up to 30%
Music	up to 60%
Physical Education	at least 60% and up to 70%
Science	at least 25% and up to 30%
Welsh	at least 30% and up to 40%
Welsh Literature	up to 30%
Welsh Second Language	up to 40%

IT SOUNDS AS THOUGH I AM GOING TO HAVE TO TAKE A LOT OF EXAMS

It depends on how you look at it.

Your ability will be tested throughout the two years. But your coursework performance will in some cases enable you to go into the examination well on your way to a good grade.

WHAT IF SIX DIFFERENT TEACHERS GIVE ME COURSEWORK AT THE SAME TIME – I'D BE A WRECK!

Coursework overload is a possible hazard of the GCSE. Your teachers will be anxious to avoid overloading you. Nobody can tackle a great number of large assignments at the same time and do them all well – and your teachers do want you to do well.

In a well-run school, coursework overload should not happen. Before the two year course begins, teachers usually get together and work out a timetable for setting coursework assignments. But even the best run systems can break down. So, be alert...if you are given too much coursework at any one time, don't worry in silence. Tell your teachers about the problem immediately.

No doubt you will find yourself working harder than you have had to before, but, remember, your teachers are not trying to work you to a standstill. It is in their interests as well as yours that you should do well.

COURSEWORK IS TO YOUR ADVANTAGE

GCSE has been widely praised for allowing candidates to demonstrate what they know, understand and can do.

Coursework allows a wider range of skills to be assessed than is possible in a written examination. Evidence suggests that coursework assessment increases candidates' motivation.

- If you are a good communicator you'll have the chance to prove it

- If you are a painstaking perfectionist you'll have the time to perfect your work and so earn marks for it

- If you are a thinker you'll have time to think

- If you are a problem solver you'll get the time to find the solution

But...

It's no good leaving everything to the last minute with GCSE. You won't get through by copying someone else's notes the day before the exam. You'll need to work throughout the two years to do well – and work hard. Sorry, but there's no escape.

WHAT IF I'M ILL WHEN AN ASSESSMENT IS DUE?

You'll find that the deadlines set for coursework are quite flexible, so the odd week, even a month of illness, should not set you back too much.

BUT WHAT IF I'M AWAY FOR A TERM OR LONGER?

Most teachers and Examining Groups are very sympathetic if you are ill and will try to find a way for you to complete the course.

There are no hard and fast rules...subjects vary, and so do individual cases. But if you have completed enough pieces of coursework over the two years, they can usually assess how well you are likely to do, and give you a fair mark. However, one thing is certain. Both your school and Examining Group want you to take the exam and will do their best to help you. So, if you know you are going to miss school for some reason, tell your teachers as soon as possible, so that they can make alternative arrangements for you.

WHAT HAPPENS IF I CHANGE SCHOOLS IN THE MIDDLE OF MY GCSE?

It should not be too difficult for you to change from a course set by one Examining Group to one set by another because they will both be assessing the same skills.

In addition, you might be able to transfer any coursework you have already completed. But – and it is a very big BUT – it depends on what subjects you are taking. The Joint Council for the GCSE certainly recommends that assessment across syllabuses from more than one Examining Group should be allowed.

For example, it is much easier to move from one syllabus to another in Maths or a Modern Foreign Language than it is, say in History, where you could be studying a different historical period. And in English Literature the set books are unlikely to be the same, so, again, transfer tends to be more difficult.

If you are well advanced in your original studies when you make the move, then arrangements can be made for you to take the exam in your original course in your new school. Your teachers and the examiners will try and do their best for each student, so your case would be treated sympathetically.

MY TEACHER DOESN'T LIKE ME. WILL IT AFFECT MY ASSESSMENT MARKS?

No.

Equally, you can't be upgraded by your teacher either. You can rest assured there will be neither discrimination nor favouritism in your GCSE assessment. No teacher would allow any personal feelings to influence the results of a public examination. Besides which, there are too many checks and safeguards...so, it couldn't happen anyway. And all research shows that coursework is no less reliable than written examinations.

WHAT'S TO STOP SOMEONE ELSE DOING MY COURSEWORK FOR ME?

The work which you submit for assessment must be your own. Teachers have to certify that coursework has been supervised properly. And teachers are usually very shrewd: they know what most of their students are capable of.

If you quote from any books or other materials, you should state which sources you have used. And, if you receive guidance from someone other than your teacher, you should tell your teacher who will then record the nature of the assistance.

SOME TEACHERS EXPECT MORE OF THEIR STUDENTS THAN OTHERS AND SO MARK STIFFLY – HOW CAN THE COURSES BE COMPLETELY FAIR?

Teachers are provided with resource packs for use in preparing coursework, together with examples of candidates' work from previous examinations to demonstrate the standards required. There are also opportunities to talk with other teachers and moderators from the Examining Groups at meetings, in order to standardise work from the current examination.

WHAT IS A MODERATOR?

The Moderator is somebody outside your school who will look at the work of your class in relation to the coursework done by other schools. If the Moderator thinks your teacher has marked too harshly or too leniently, compared with other teachers, then the marks will be adjusted to bring them into line. So the system is doubly fair because more than one person will be marking your work.

WILL I KNOW WHAT MARKS I GET FOR MY COURSEWORK?

Your school might tell you how well you have done in individual pieces of work, but you are unlikely to be told your overall coursework mark – after all, the moderator system may see it changed.

5. THE EXAM UNDER EXAMINATION

After you've put in all the hard work over two years, what about the last hurdle – the exam itself?

Probably the greatest difference between school examinations and the GCSE examinations is *time*. In most schools, the end of year exams are concentrated into approximately two weeks, maybe less. This is possible because most schools do not offer a very large number of subjects. So the exams come thick and fast, often two or three in a day.

It's very different with the GCSE. Exams are spread over a much longer period of time – so you should find that your exams are well spaced out with free days in between. Great – more time for revision! But then you may need more time because you'll be tested on two years' work. The timetable for exams is drawn up well in advance, so you should know the term before the exams start when you will actually sit each paper.

WHEN I COME TO TAKE MY EXAMS WILL SUBJECTS CLASH ON THE TIMETABLE?

Each year the six Examining Groups get together and draw up a common timetable to avoid possible clashes of exams for students taking subjects from different Groups.

WILL WE REALLY ALL DO THE SAME EXAM PAPERS?

No. In most subjects, alternative papers exist and teachers, supported by Examining Groups, are responsible for ensuring that students are entered for papers which set appropriate targets. This is in addition to the different types and levels of work that students undertake in coursework, which is also chosen in consultation with teachers.

In most cases, students will actually sit different papers according to their own abilities. This process is known as 'tiering' and the common model that has emerged is of one paper that is intended for students expected to achieve in the range A* to D and another, overlapping tier for those who are more likely to be awarded grades C to G.

In Maths, there are three overlapping tiers, one for starred A* to C, one for B to E and one for D to G.

In Art, Music, History and Physical Education, questions can be set which allow all students to respond effectively at their own level. Examination papers are therefore designed to cover the full grade range, without the need for tiering.

Coursework is another way of enabling candidates to demonstrate differentiated ability, with the additional advantages of an unpressured environment and access to guidance from a teacher.

IT ALL SOUNDS A BIT COMPLICATED TO ME!

If it sounds a complicated system, don't worry. Before you get anywhere near taking the exams, your teacher will tell you which kind of paper you will be taking in each subject. They will also probably show you examples of what the exam papers will look like and you'll have a chance to try them out. Don't worry, you will be in no doubt about what to do, and what's expected of you when you take the exam.

I JUST CAN'T DO EXAMS, I GO TO PIECES. IS IT WORTH ME BOTHERING?

Take heart, the GCSE does help people like you. If you choose the subjects that best suit you, work consistently and well at your coursework and then revise thoroughly for the final examination, you could surprise yourself.

IS THE GCSE GIVING ME A GOOD DEAL?

Most people think so and here are the reasons why:

- It is fair because it tests all your skills

- The courses are interesting and relevant

- Everybody has the same chance of success because you all take the same exam and succeed at your own level.

6. CHOOSING THE RIGHT SUBJECTS

SUBJECTS THAT CAN BE TAKEN AT GCSE

Accounting
Agricultural Science
American Studies
Applied Science
Arabic
Archaeology
Art
Art & Design

Bengali
Biblical Hebrew
Biology
Biology (Human)
British Government & Politics
British Industrial Society
Building Studies
Business Studies
Business & Information Studies

Catering
CDT: Design & Communication
CDT: Design & Realisation
CDT: Technology
Chemistry
Chinese
Classical Civilisation
Classical Subjects: Latin
Classical Subjects: Greek
Commerce
Communication Studies
Community Issues
Computer Studies
Control Technology

Creative Arts
Critical Studies in Art & Design

Dance
Design
Design & Communication
Design & Realisation
Design & Technology
Design Centred Studies
Drama
Drama & Theatre Arts
Drama: Community Theatre

Economics
Electronics
Engineering Workshop Theory and Practice
English
English Literature
Environmental Science
Environmental Studies
European Arts
European Studies
Expressive Arts

French
French (Modular)

General Studies
Geography
Geology
German
German (Modular)
Graphic & Technical Communication
Graphic Communication
Greek
Greek Civilisation
Gujarati

Hindi
History
History (Britain, Europe & the World 19th/20th C)
History (British 19th & 20th C)

History (British & European)
History (Economic & Social)
History (British, Social & Economic)
History (English History 16th & 17th C)
History (Modern World/20th C)
History (Social and Industrial History of England & Wales,
18th & 19th C)
Home Economics
Home Economics: Child Development
Home Economics: Family, Home & Food
Home Economics: Food
Home Economics: Home and Family
Home Economics: Textiles
Humanities

Information Studies
Information Systems
Information Technology
Integrated Humanities
Italian

Japanese

Keyboarding Applications

Land Surveying
Latin
Latin & Roman Civilisation
Law
Law in Society

Marine Navigation
Mathematics
Mathematics (SMP)
Mathematical Studies
Media Studies
Modern Greek
Modern Hebrew
Modular Mathematics
Modular Science
Motor Vehicle Studies
Music

Nautical Studies
Navigation

Office Skills
Office Studies
Office Technology

Panjabi
Persian
Photography
Physical Education
Physics
Polish
Political Studies
Politics & Government
Portuguese
Psychology
Psychology (Child Development)

Religious Studies
Religious Studies (Islam)
Rural Science
Russian
Russian Studies

Science (Single Award and Double Award)
Science (Biology, Chemistry and Physics)
Science (Geology, Rural and Environmental)
Science, Technology & Society
Social Science
Sociology
Spanish
Statistics
Surveying

Technical Communication
Technology
Technology & Organisations
Textiles
Turkish

Ukrainian
Understanding Industrial Society
Urdu

Welfare & Society
Welsh
Welsh Literature
Welsh Second Language
World Development

HOW TO CHOOSE THE RIGHT SUBJECTS

Because young people frequently change their career ideas at this stage, most schools have always put some restrictions on choice of subject. The introduction of the National Curriculum has gone much further in ensuring that you keep your options open by not specialising too narrowly at an early stage.

The National Curriculum has greatly limited the number of choices that have to be made by young people during Year 9 (Year 10 in Northern Ireland), but when there are still choices to be made, how should you set about choosing?

1. Ask yourself:

What do I want to do when I leave school?

a. If you know exactly what career you want to follow then turn to Chapter 8 and see what GCSE subjects are required.

b. If you are thinking of studying for a degree then take a look at a degree course guide – *Degree Course Offers* by Brian Heap (now also available on CD-ROM) is excellent as it gives details of the subjects required for different higher education courses.

c. If you've no idea, don't worry. You are probably in the majority... 13 or 14 is an early age to decide on a career. Your aim now should be to choose a selection of subjects that will keep as many career doors open as possible.

2. Ask yourself:

What am I good at ?

AND

What do I enjoy doing?

Are any of the available GCSE subjects closely related to these interests?

Now add any subjects that you think are essential to your chosen career. Already you are beginning to get a list.

3. Ask yourself:

Which subjects are most likely to be on offer at my school?

Here is a list of the subjects most likely to be offered by schools:

MATHS	HUMANITIES
ENGLISH	Geography
Language	History
Literature	Religious Education
SCIENCES	EXPRESSIVE ARTS
Biology	Art
Chemistry	Dance
Physics	Drama
Science	Music
Single or Double Award	MODERN LANGUAGES
TECHNOLOGY	French
Business Studies	German
Design & Technology	Spanish
Information Technology	

4. Ask yourself:

What about other options?

Before you make your final choice, remember – the GCSE offers a range of subjects you've probably never tried before. Many schools will organise a few sample lessons in the 'new' subjects they offer, to give you some idea of what they are like. These subjects could be useful, even a deciding factor to your future career, so give them serious consideration.

You may well now have a list as long as your arm, so the next question must be:

5. Ask yourself:

How many subjects should I take?

As many as you are capable of doing **well**. Most people would say that getting a G in nine subjects isn't as good as getting a D or C in six. It is well worth listening to the advice of your teachers about striking the right balance.

COURSEWORK OVERLOAD

Don't overburden yourself with coursework.

Some subjects involve more research-based coursework to be done outside the classroom than others. History and Geography are good examples of this. Maths and Modern Foreign Languages, on the other hand, will probably include very little. As it is important to make sure you have sufficient time to do every project well, and so do justice to your ability, make sure you get the workload right by **not** choosing too many subjects that are heavy on coursework. So, check coursework content with your teachers.

WHAT ARE MODULAR COURSES?

Modular schemes offer young people the opportunity to study relatively small parts of the curriculum in a concentrated period. Each unit or module contains very specific and understandable learning targets, with the student's learning assessed at the end of each module.

The different structure of modular courses, with a heavy emphasis on assessment and systematic feedback between teacher and student, suits some students better than the more traditional structure, even though GCSE courses have been reformed to contain these elements.

In future, the emphasis on terminal examinations will broadly apply to modular courses also. In most subjects except Design & Technology, at least 60% of the marks will come from terminal examinations; end-of-unit tests which count towards the final assessment will be externally set and marked; and any marks allocated for coursework will be set at the same limit as for the ordinary GCSE in that subject.

AND FINALLY

Your teachers will see it as part of their responsibility to see that you are entered for the most appropriate subjects and syllabuses available. So, before opting for, or committing yourself, to any course, make sure that you ask each subject teacher:

- how much reading is involved
- how much writing is involved
- how much coursework is involved
- what percentage of the marks is given for coursework
- if there's the option of different tiers of assessment
- if there's an oral test
- if you'll have to gather information for yourself
- if projects are involved
- what practical skills are involved
- how much laboratory or fieldwork is involved.

Armed with this information, you should be well placed to begin to make your GCSE decisions.

7. BEFORE YOU MAKE UP YOUR MIND

Before you make your final selection, here are a few more questions that might occur to you.

ARE ALL THE GCSE SUBJECTS RECOGNISED BY EMPLOYERS, PROFESSIONAL BODIES, UNIVERSITIES AND COLLEGES OF FURTHER EDUCATION?

The short answer is 'no'. If a minimum number of GCSEs is required by such people, they will sometimes not accept creative and expressive subjects like Art and Music.

The advice is *CHECK YOUR OPTIONS ARE SUITABLE FOR YOUR LONG TERM PLANS.*

But don't get the idea that subjects like Art and Music are not good courses to take. They are. It depends on what you want to do. For example, if you are thinking of becoming a graphic designer or an architect, then you should take Art. And that is quite apart from the value of such subjects in helping you develop a broader range of personal skills and interests.

WHY DO EMPLOYERS AND COLLEGES OFTEN ASK FOR FIVE SUBJECTS TAKEN ALL AT ONE TIME?

By asking for five subjects at one sitting, employers can expect you to be capable of coping with a lot of sustained work. It gives them a better idea of your all-round ability.

WHAT ARE 'ACADEMIC' SUBJECTS?

You'll hear people use the term 'academic subjects'. They are referring to subjects that are considered to involve more theoretical work, rather than practical skills. This distinction is no longer a helpful one, since it creates an artificial divide between the 'academic' subjects and the practical and 'vocational' courses. GCSE has put increasing emphasis on relevance and practical skills, while most of the subjects labelled 'practical' or 'vocational' are intellectually demanding in at least some of their components.

WHAT CAN I DO IF THE GCSE SUBJECT I WANT TO DO IS NOT OFFERED AT MY SCHOOL?

The best advice is to wait until you are 16, when you'll probably be able to find it at a college, where the range of subjects offered is often much wider. In fact, many sixth form teachers and tutors suggest students take an additional GCSE as well as A-levels or other courses they may be taking. If, however, you want to take the subject before then, you may be able to find a specialist tutor, although this will not always be easy.

CAN YOU GET THE TOP GRADE IN ALL SUBJECTS?

Yes.

But only if your syllabuses have been designed to include all the work necessary for the top grade or level to be awarded. If it is more appropriate to your needs, the syllabus in particular subjects may be designed so that the work involved will earn, at the highest, a grade C. Similarly, it is possible for syllabuses to be designed so that the lowest level that can be awarded for the work involved is a grade E: see the paragraphs on tiering in Chapter 5.

Your teacher would tell you if a course you will be doing involves all the work required for the top level awards or if it is restricted in some way.

It is also important to remember that if you opt for an exam on high-level papers with, say grade C as the lowest level available, you are NOT guaranteed that minimum. If you fail to achieve that minimum standard, you will be UNGRADED.

WHY DO I HAVE TO START SELECTING MY GCSE SUBJECTS SO EARLY IN YEAR 9 (YEAR 10 IN NORTHERN IRELAND)?

A large school might well have over 200 students in one year, choosing from quite a few different subjects. Drawing up a timetable to suit everyone, including the students and the teachers, is a major task. These days most schools make at least some use of a computer, but it still takes time.

WHAT'S A DOUBLE AWARD?

The most common example is in Science. Most schools now opt to give all students a broad and balanced science curriculum, rather than just one or two of the traditional Science subjects – Biology, Physics and Chemistry. Some of the syllabuses offered count as two subjects – in other words, a 'double award'.

8. CHOOSING THE RIGHT GCSEs FOR YOUR CAREER

This guide will tell you the GCSEs you should consider studying if you have a certain career, or possibly several careers, in mind.

There are different ways of getting into many careers – but the usual method for most careers, and the ONLY way for many, is through a RECOGNISED TRAINING COURSE OR A DEGREE, PROFESSIONAL OR OTHER COURSE.

There are other less rigid forms of entry to some careers. You will always hear about people who have succeeded in different walks of life without qualifications. But they are the exceptions. For the vast majority of us the only way is through qualifications.

To check the qualifications you will need, this is what you do:

- Look up all the careers that interest you.
- Write down all the GCSE subjects required.
- Make a list of all the different subjects mentioned.

This will give you a good base on which to build your choice of subject.

The information given for each occupation in the following section is as follows:

NAME OF JOB
ENTRY LEVELS
The points at which entry is possible for school/college leavers.

The codes used are:

N	=	No qualifications necessary.
G	=	GCSEs (or S grades) expected, but no specific grades.
G+	=	GCSEs at grades A-C (or S grades 1-3)
GD	=	Full-time diploma or other training course which is entered after GCSEs (or S grades), eg BTEC/SCOTVEC National Diploma.
A	=	1 or more A-levels.
AD	=	Full-time diploma or degree which is entered after A-levels or BTEC/SCOTVEC National, eg BTEC/SCOTVEC Higher National Diploma or BA/BSc degree.

GCSEs normally required	=	Numbers required or any specific subjects required or preferred.
GCSEs which may be useful	=	These are subjects which you may wish to consider taking as they can be helpful, but are not essential.
Other academic/training requirements	=	Full-time study beyond GCSE level which is needed before entering the career – eg A-levels, secretarial course, National Diploma, degree, etc.
Personality/physical requirements	=	Any special considerations in addition to academic qualifications.

WHAT IS A 'GOOD SPREAD' OF GCSEs?

A good spread of GCSEs usually means five or more subjects, all at grade C or above (or S grades at 3 or above in Scotland).

Although we have made some mention of Scottish equivalents (eg S grades and SCOTVEC), the position in Scotland is substantially different. For example, the Scottish Higher system is different from A-levels in England and Wales, while there are also different career structures for some professions in Scotland. As a consequence, Scottish readers (or those anticipating a career in Scotland) are advised to seek more detailed information, where it seems appropriate.

I'M THINKING ABOUT A LEGAL CAREER

BARRISTER
Entry levels: AD.
GCSEs normally required: Usually 5 GCSEs at grade C or above. English required.
GCSEs which may be useful: History, modern languages.
Other academic/training requirements: Degree is essential, some advantage in a law degree – selectors at certain law schools may prefer arts/social science A-levels. For those wishing to practise in Scotland, a law degree should be taken at a Scottish university).
Personality/physical requirements: Communications skills; analytical ability; ability to argue a case; logic and clear-thinking capabilities; a good voice is advantageous.

BARRISTER'S CLERK
Entry levels: G+, A, AD.
GCSEs normally required: 4 at grade C or above, including English and Mathematics.
GCSEs which may be useful: IT.
Other academic/training requirements: None before entry.
Personality/physical requirements: Ability to organise, discretion.

LEGAL EXECUTIVE
Entry levels: G+, A.
GCSEs normally required: 4 at grade C or above. English required, other subjects must be academic – technical and craft subjects are not accepted.
GCSEs which may be useful: Business studies.
Other academic/training requirements: A-levels (or equivalent) sometimes preferred.
Personality/physical requirements: Organising ability; logic.

LEGAL SECRETARY

Entry levels: G+, GD, A.

GCSEs normally required: Generally 3 or 4 at grade C or above, including English.

GCSEs which may be useful: Business studies, IT.

Other academic/training requirements: Secretarial course. A-levels may be advantageous.

Personality/physical requirements: Pleasant manner; ability to organise; discretion.

SOLICITOR

Entry levels: AD.

GCSEs normally required: 5 GCSEs at grade C or above. English required.

GCSEs which may be useful: Modern languages, history.

Other academic/training requirements: Entry after A-level is no longer possible. Some advantage in taking a law degree – selectors at certain schools prefer arts/social science A-levels (in Scotland H grade in English, plus maths or a science or a foreign language).

Personality/physical requirements: communications skills; ability to argue a case; clear thinking capabilities.

See also – *I'M THINKING ABOUT A CAREER IN SECURITY*

I'M THINKING ABOUT A CAREER IN 'THE GREAT OUTDOORS'

FARM MANAGER

Entry levels: GD, AD.

GCSEs normally required: 4 GCSEs at grade C or above, to include English and 2 maths/science subjects.

GCSEs which may be useful: Business studies.

Other academic/training requirements: Diploma entered after GCSEs or A-levels(including a science); or degree. Practical experience required before diploma/degree in each case.

Personality/physical requirements: Fitness, organising ability; business sense; scientific interest.

FARMWORKER

Entry levels: N, G.
GCSEs normally required: None specified, but GCSEs may help.
GCSEs which may be useful: English, maths, science, practical
subjects.
Other academic/training requirements: None before entry.
Personality/physical requirements: Fitness; strength; ability to
endure bad weather; able to work with little supervision; sense
of responsibility; mechanical aptitude; good with animals.

FISH FARMER

Entry levels: G+, GD, AD.
GCSEs normally required: 4 or more GCSEs at grade C or above.
Double science (or equivalent) preferred.
Other academic/training requirements: Diplomas are now available
after GCSEs or science A-levels; science-based degrees also offered.
Personality/physical requirements: Fitness; organising ability.

FISHER

Entry levels: N, G.
GCSEs normally required: No special requirements.
GCSEs which may be useful: Nautical studies, geography.
Other academic/training requirements: None before entry.
Personality/physical requirements: Physical fitness and strength;
courage; ability to endure harsh weather; good at team work.

FOREST OFFICER

Entry levels: GD, AD.
GCSEs normally required: 4 GCSEs at grade C or above, to include
English, maths and science.
GCSEs which may be useful: Environmental science, geography.
Other academic/training requirements: Diploma entered after GCSEs
and practical experience; or forestry degree (needs science A-levels).
Practical experience helpful before entry into some training routes.
Personality/physical requirements: Fitness; organising ability; business
sense for commercial forestry.

FOREST WORKER

Entry levels: N, G.

GCSEs normally required: None specified but GCSEs helpful because of competition for jobs.

GCSEs which may be useful: Science, practical subjects.

Other academic/training requirements: None before entry.

Personality/physical requirements: Fitness; strength; ability to endure bad weather; care in handling plants; safety conscious; mechanical aptitude; able to work alone and unsupervised.

GAMEKEEPER

Entry levels: N, G.

GCSEs normally required: No formal qualifications needed but GCSEs may help because of competition.

GCSEs which may be useful: Sciences (particularly for biology, rural science, environmental science content), practical subjects.

Other academic/training requirements: None before entry.

Personality/physical requirements: Fitness; ability to work alone and unsupervised; sense of responsibility; carefulness in handling young birds etc; willingness to learn to drive and shoot; versatility.

GARDENER

Entry levels: N, G.

GCSEs normally required: None specified.

GCSEs which may be useful: Sciences (particularly for biology, rural science, environmental science content).

Other academic/training requirements: None before entry.

Personality/physical requirements: Reasonable fitness; tidy workmanship; care in handling plants; eye for design and colour; ability to work with little supervision and alone.

HORTICULTURAL MANAGER

Entry levels: GD, AD.

GCSEs normally required: 4 or more at grade C or above, to include English (or English subject) and 2 maths or science subjects.

GCSEs which may be useful: Business studies, geography.

Other academic/training requirements: Either BTEC National diploma after GCSEs; or BTEC Higher National Diploma or degree after A-levels (including a science).

Personality/physical requirements: Reasonable fitness; organising ability; business sense for commercial horticulture; eye for design/colour for amenity horticulture; scientific interest.

HORTICULTURAL WORKER
Entry levels: N, G, G+.
GCSEs normally required: Some preference for people with GCSEs, especially in science subjects.
Other academic/training requirements: None before entry.
Personality/physical requirements: Fitness and stamina; mechanical aptitude to deal with motorised equipment; care in handling plants and crops.

LANDSCAPE ARCHITECT
Entry levels: AD.
GCSEs normally required: 5 GCSEs at grade C or above, including English, maths or science, and either history or geography or a foreign language.
GCSEs which may be useful: Art, biology, botany, design and technology, environmental science, geology.
Other academic/training requirements: Diploma or degree in landscape architecture, for which A-levels (eg in subjects mentioned above) are needed.
Personality/physical requirements: Creative or design ability; good communications skills; practical but imaginative outlook; interest in environment.

PARK KEEPER/GROUNDS STAFF
Entry levels: N, G.
GCSEs normally required: None specified but they may help, of course.
GCSEs which may be useful: Sciences.
Other academic/training requirements: None before entry.
Personality/physical requirements: Ability to work alone and unsupervised; ability to put up with bad weather; tidy workmanship.

See also – *I'M THINKING ABOUT A CAREER IN SCIENCE*
for Agricultural and Horticultural Scientist and for Environmental Scientist/Ecologist.

I'M THINKING ABOUT A CAREER WORKING WITH ANIMALS

BLACKSMITH
Entry levels: N, G.
GCSEs normally required: Good general education but no special requirements.
GCSEs which may be useful: Maths, design and technology, engineering, science, practical subjects.
Other academic/training requirements: None before entry.
Personality/physical requirements: Interest in horses; strength and fitness; manual dexterity; patience.

GROOM/STABLEHAND
Entry levels: N, G, G+.
GCSEs normally required: No set qualifications but if you have some GCSEs, you may take equestrian exams.
GCSEs which may be useful: Sciences (particularly for biology, zoology content).
Other academic/training requirements: None before entry.
Personality/physical requirements: Fitness and energy; real love of horses.

HORSE RIDING INSTRUCTOR
Entry levels: N, G, G+.
GCSEs normally required: For qualified instructor, 4 GCSEs at grade C or above, including English.
GCSEs which may be useful: Sciences (particularly for biology, zoology content).
Other academic/training requirements: None before entry.
Personality/physical requirements: Good at handling people, especially children; patience; real love for horses; fitness.

KENNEL WORKER
Entry levels: N, G.
GCSEs normally required: GCSEs are an advantage.
GCSEs which may be useful: Sciences (particularly for biology, zoology content).

Other academic/training requirements: None before entry.
Personality/physical requirements: Fitness and energy; good
observation skills; genuine love of dogs; sense of responsibility.

VETERINARY NURSE
Entry levels: G, G+.
GCSEs normally required: To qualify for the Royal College of
Veterinary Surgeons (RCVS) Veterinary Nursing Scheme, 4 GCSEs
at grade C or above, to include English language, and maths or
science.
GCSEs which may be useful: Biology, zoology.
Other academic/training requirements: Genuine caring for animals,
without sentimentality; lack of squeamishness; sense of
responsibility; good with owners as well as animals. Applicants for
the RCVS Scheme must have at least promise of paid employment
at an approved training centre.

VETERINARY SURGEON
Entry levels: AD.
GCSEs normally required: Good spread of GCSEs, at least at grade
C. Entry is very competitive and high academic qualifications are
needed. Subjects – English, maths, double science (or equivalent).
Other academic/training requirements: Veterinary degree is essential –
this requires very good science A-levels.
Personality/physical requirements: Scientific interest; manual
dexterity; good observational skills; fitness and energy; caring but
unsentimental approach to animals.

ZOO KEEPER
Entry levels: N, G, G+.
GCSEs normally required: No set qualification but this is a
competitive area, and GCSEs may help you to get a job and,
later, promotion.
GCSEs which may be useful: English, maths, science, geography, a
foreign language, practical subjects.
Other academic/training requirements: None before entry.
Personality/physical requirements: Fitness and energy; good
observation skills; sense of responsibility; true interest in animals.

See also – *I'M THINKING ABOUT A CAREER IN THE 'GREAT OUTDOORS'* for farming careers

I'M THINKING ABOUT A CAREER IN TRANSPORT OR TRAVEL

AIR CABIN CREW

Entry levels: G+, A.

GCSEs normally required: Preferably several GCSEs at grade C or above. Preferred subjects are modern languages, English, maths.

GCSEs which may be useful: Geography, home economics/food studies, child care.

Other academic/training requirements: Experience in a job dealing with people – eg nursing, care work, catering. A-levels can be advantageous.

Personality/physical requirements: Minimum height requirement of about 1.57m to 1.62m and weight in proportion to height, normal colour vision and, usually, good eyesight. Ability to swim normally required. Good appearance, calm and pleasant manner; clear speaking voice. Minimum age of 19 upwards.

DRIVER (Bus, Taxi, Lorry etc)

Entry levels: N, G.

GCSEs normally required: No special requirements normally.

GCSEs which may be useful: Motor vehicle studies.

Other academic/training requirements: You'll need at least a car driving licence pre-entry.

Personality/physical requirements: Good health and character; some mechanical aptitude can be an advantage; good concentration; good manner with people, if you work with the public.

MERCHANT NAVY DECK OFFICER

Entry levels: G+, A, AD.

GCSEs normally required: Minimum of 4 GCSEs at grade C or above, to include maths, science and a subject involving the use of English.

GCSEs which may be useful: Nautical studies, design and technology, geography.

Other academic/training requirements: Entry possible after GCSEs, maths/science A-levels or suitable degree.

Personality/physical requirements: Very good health, fitness and vision (including colour); strong sense of responsibility; qualities of leadership; mathematical and scientific abilities; able to mix well with shipmates and endure long voyages in the same company.

MERCHANT NAVY DECK/CATERING RATING

Entry levels: G.

GCSEs normally required: A minimum of 3 GCSEs or equivalent, in maths, science and a subject showing the use of English.

GCSEs which may be useful: Nautical studies, home economics/food studies for catering trainees.

Other academic/training requirements: None before entry.

Personality/physical requirements: Fitness; good vision for deck ratings; safety consciousness and sense of responsibility; practical/mechanical skills. Able to get on well with shipmates at work and socially.

MERCHANT NAVY ENGINEERING OFFICER

Entry levels: G+, A, AD.

GCSEs normally required: 4 GCSEs at grade C or above, including maths, science and a subject involving the use of English. GCSEs which may be useful: nautical studies, design and technology.

Other academic/training requirements: Entry is possible after GCSEs, or after A-levels (preferably maths and physics) or suitable degree.

Personality/physical requirements: Mechanical and scientific abilities; good at teamwork; able to cope with possible boredom/monotony of life at sea; good vision (with glasses if worn) and good colour vision.

RAILWAY FITTER/ELECTRICIAN

Entry levels: G, G+.

GCSEs normally required: GCSEs in English, maths and science are desirable.

GCSEs which may be useful: Design and technology, engineering.

Other academic/training requirements: None before entry.

Personality/physical requirements: Physical fitness, technical/mechanical abilities.

49

ROAD TRANSPORT MANAGER
Entry levels: A, AD.
GCSEs normally required: For direct entry at management level –
5 GCSEs at grade C or above, to include English and maths.
GCSEs which may be useful: Economics, business studies, IT.
Other academic/training requirements: A-levels and, often, a degree.
Personality/physical requirements: Organising ability; business sense.

TRAVEL AGENCY WORK
Entry levels: G+, GD, A, AD.
GCSEs normally required: Usually about 4 GCSEs at grade C or
above. English and maths preferred.
GCSEs which may be useful: Modern languages, geography,
business studies, IT.
Other academic/training requirements: Entry possible at various points
– after GCSEs, A-levels or degree, or after suitable diploma/higher
diploma course with travel option.
Personality/physical requirements: Good organising abilities; business
sense; pleasant manner with people – diplomatic.

TRAVEL COURIER/RESORT REPRESENTATIVE
Entry levels: G, G+, A.
GCSEs normally required: No special qualifications, but good
GCSEs are advantageous, as competition for jobs is fierce. Modern
languages preferred.
GCSEs which may be useful: English, maths, geography.
Other academic/training requirements: None before entry, though
A-levels can be advantageous.
Personality/physical requirements: Good organising ability; pleasant
and helpful manner with people.

I'M THINKING ABOUT A CAREER IN THE FORCES

ARMY – SOLDIERS AND SERVICE WOMEN
Entry levels: N, G, G+.
GCSEs normally required: No special qualifications – but some
GCSEs, especially maths, science, design shod technology, etc may

make it easier to enter certain specialist areas.

GCSEs which may be useful: See above.

Other academic/training requirements: None before entry.

Personality/physical requirements: Physical fitness; good attitude to discipline and communal life; safety consciousness.

ARMY OFFICER

Entry levels: G, A, AD.

GCSEs normally required: Depends on the type of commission. Generally, minimum of 5 GCSEs at grade C or above, to include English, maths and science or a foreign language.

GCSEs which may be useful: See above.

Other academic/training requirements: Most opportunities require at least 2 A-levels and/or a degree.

Personality/physical requirements: Qualities of leadership; fitness; self confidence and ability to inspire confidence in others; clear thinking and well-organised; liking for communal life; smart appearance.

RAF AIRMAN/AIRWOMAN

Entry levels: N, G, G+.

GCSEs normally required: Depends on branch. No special requirements for some trades. Technicians, technician apprentices, air engineer/electronics operators: 2-4 GCSEs at grade C or above, including maths, science and preferably English. Air engineer, air loadmaster and air electronics operator: 3 GCSEs at grade C or above, including English, maths and a science.

GCSEs which may be useful: Depends upon branch. Sciences generally useful.

Other academic/training requirements: None before entry.

Personality/physical requirements: Fitness; good attitude to discipline; safety consciousness and common sense; practical and technical interests for many trades; liking for teamwork and communal life.

RAF OFFICER

Entry levels: A, AD.

GCSEs normally required: Depends on the branch, but should include English language and maths. Generally, minimum of 5 GCSEs at grade C or above. Science advantageous for many specialisms.

GCSEs which may be useful: See above.

Other academic/training requirements: A-levels and/or a higher diploma/degree.

Personality/physical requirements: Fitness, qualities of leadership; self confidence and ability to inspire confidence in others; good organisational abilities; liking for communal life; smart appearance.

ROYAL MARINES

Entry levels: N, G, G+.

GCSEs normally required: None. Selection test involves reasoning, English language, numeracy and mechanical comprehension.

GCSEs which may be useful: See above.

Other academic/training requirements: None before entry.

Personality/physical requirements: Fitness; good attitude to discipline; good at teamwork; safety consciousness; practical attitude; liking for communal life and able to endure long periods at sea; able to swim. Musical aptitude in case of musician entry.

ROYAL NAVY/WRNS RATINGS

Entry levels: N, G, G+.

GCSEs normally required: Depends on the specialism. Many require no special qualifications, but technical specialises require 1, 2 or more GCSEs at grade C or above, to include English, maths and science. Medical technicians require 5 GCSEs.

GCSEs which may be useful: Scientific and technical/practical subjects generally.

Other academic/training requirements: None before entry.

Personality/physical requirements: Fitness; good attitude to discipline; good at teamwork; safety consciousness; practical attitude; liking for communal life and able to endure long periods at sea; able to swim.

ROYAL NAVY AND ROYAL MARINES OFFICER

Entry levels: G+, A, AD.
GCSEs normally required: 5 GCSEs at grade C or above, including English and maths.
GCSEs which may be useful: Science, languages.
Other academic/training requirements: A-levels normally required; graduate entry also available.
Personality/physical requirements: Qualities of leadership; fitness; smart appearance; liking for teamwork and communal living.

I'M THINKING ABOUT A CAREER IN ENTERTAINMENT OR PERFORMING

ACTOR/ACTRESS

Entry levels: N, G, G+, GD, A, AD.
GCSEs normally required: No specific requirements – but GCSEs (preferably 5 at grade C or above) required by some drama schools and for all drama degree courses.
GCSEs which may be useful: English literature, drama, music.
Other academic/training requirements: Real talent is essential – the profession is overcrowded. A-levels needed for degree courses. Advisable to have a 'second career' to take up while 'resting'.
Personality/physical requirements: Stamina; imagination; good speaking voice; persistence. Ability to cope with a difficult lifestyle, often involving travel.

BOX OFFICE STAFF

Entry levels: N, G.
GCSEs normally required: No specific requirements. Maths may be preferred.
GCSEs which may be useful: Office skills subjects.
Other academic/training requirements: None before entry.
Personality/physical requirements: Ability to deal with members of the public; ability to cope with being very busy; numeracy – to handle money and give change.

CAMERA OPERATOR (TV)

Entry levels: G+.
GCSEs normally required: No specific requirements, but advantageous to offer at least 3 GCSEs at grade C or above, including English, maths and science (with physics content).
GCSEs which may be useful: Technical subjects.
Other academic/training requirements: Experience with sound recording equipment and microphones.
Personality/physical requirements: Good hearing; technical/practical interests; patience.

DANCER

Entry levels: N, G, G+, GD, A, AD.
GCSEs normally required: No specific requirements – but GCSEs (preferably 5 at grade C or above) preferred by many dance schools and required for dance degree courses.
GCSEs which may be useful: Music, drama.
Other academic/training requirements: Real talent is essential for either classical or modern dance and training usually begins in childhood. A-levels needed for degree courses.
Personality/physical requirements: Fitness, energy and stamina; not too tall if female. Ability to cope with a difficult lifestyle, often including travel.

FASHION/PHOTOGRAPHIC MODEL

Entry levels: N, G.
GCSEs normally required: No formal qualifications; some GCSEs an advantage and 3 GCSEs necessary for eg London College of Fashion course.
GCSEs which may be useful: Drama.
Other academic/training requirements: None before entry.
Personality/physical requirements: Stamina and energy; good height and very slim build; photogenic features; self confidence; something to make you 'stand out'.

FILM EDITOR (TV)

Entry levels: A, AD.

GCSEs normally required: Good spread of GCSEs at grade C or above, to include maths and preferably science.

GCSEs which may be useful: Art, drama.

Other academic/training requirements: A-level standard of education is expected and a post-A level film course would be an advantage.

Personality/physical requirements: Serious interest in film.

FLOOR/STAGE MANAGER

Entry levels: G, G+, GD, A, AD.

GCSEs normally required: No particular requirements, but courses in stage management require 5 GCSEs at grade C or above.

GCSEs which may be useful: Art, design and technology, drama, English, English literature.

Other academic/training requirements: Pre-entry courses are available (including a wide range of degree courses in related subjects).

Personality/physical requirements: Good organising ability; versatility; fitness and energy.

LIGHTING TECHNICIAN (Theatre)

Entry levels: G, G+, GD.

GCSEs normally required: Good general education – GCSEs at grade C or above, likely to be preferred. Science, maths and design and technology subjects are preferred.

GCSEs which may be useful: Art, drama.

Other academic/training requirements: May first train as an electrician. Some full-time theatre lighting courses are available.

Personality/physical requirements: Practical/technical skills; genuine interest in theatrical work; reasonable fitness; versatility.

MAKE-UP ARTIST

Entry levels: G+, A, AD.

GCSEs normally required: Good range of GCSEs at grade C or above. English, art preferred.

GCSEs which may be useful: Science, history, drama.

Other academic/training requirements: Hairdressing and/or beauty therapy qualifications required before entry. A-level standard of education preferred.

Personality/physical requirements: Good skills with people; artistic flair; practical skills; good eyesight and colour vision.

PROFESSIONAL SPORTSMAN/WOMAN

Entry levels: N, G.

GCSEs normally required: No specific requirements – sporting skill is most important aspect.

GCSEs which may be useful: A good spread of GCSEs will be useful for the career you are likely to need to take up in later life.

Other academic/training requirements: You are likely to be 'spotted' before leaving school, in most sports.

Personality/physical requirements: Fitness, energy and stamina; willingness to accept discipline of training schedules, etc.

SINGER/MUSICIAN

Entry levels: N, G, G+, A, AD.

GCSEs normally required: No specific requirements, especially for popular music, but for courses in classical music, a good spread of GCSEs at grade C or above, is usually required.

GCSEs which may be useful: Music, drama.

Other academic/training requirements: None for popular music. Usually music college training for classical singing – A-levels (including music) may be preferred.

Personality/physical requirements: Stamina and energy; ability to cope with a difficult lifestyle, often involving travel. Persistence – this is a competitive area of work.

SOUND TECHNICIAN/OPERATOR (Film/TV)

Entry levels: G+, GD, AD

GCSEs normally required: At least 3 GCSEs at grade C or above, to include English language, maths and science.

GCSEs which may be useful: Technical subjects.

Other academic/training requirements: A relevant BTEC certificate or diploma at National or Higher level or a BA music tonmeister qualification – either necessary or desirable, dependent on entry scheme. Experience with sound recording equipment and microphones.

Personality/physical requirements: Good hearing; technical/practical interests; patience.

SPORTS/LEISURE CENTRE MANAGER

Entry levels: G+, GD, A, AD.
GCSEs normally required: Usually about 5 GCSEs at grade C or above, preferably including English and maths.
GCSEs which may be useful: Science; business studies.
Other academic/training requirements: Although entry with GCSEs is possible, jobs go increasingly to people with a recognised qualification in recreational management, eg at BTEC national or degree level.
Personality/physical requirements: Good organisational abilities; interest/ability in sport; willingness to work unsocial hours.

STUDIO MANAGER (Radio)

Entry levels: AD.
GCSEs normally required: Good spread of GCSEs, preferably including English and science.
GCSEs which may be useful: Practical subjects.
Other academic/training requirements: Preference for candidates with experience in sound recording or radio (eg local, hospital or campus radio).
Personality/physical requirements: Organised approach to work. Reasonable technical aptitudes.

STAGE DESIGNER

Entry levels: AD.
GCSEs normally required: Good spread of GCSEs at grade C or above. Art and design subjects expected.
GCSEs which may be useful: Drama.
Other academic/training requirements: Course in theatre/stage design, taken either after A-levels or a basic art training.
Personality/physical requirements: Real interest in the theatre; strong visual imagination.

I'M THINKING ABOUT A CAREER IN SECURITY

FIREFIGHTER
Entry levels: N, G, G+.
GCSEs normally required: No formal requirements, but some GCSEs preferred, especially English, maths and science.
GCSEs which may be useful: Practical subjects.
Other academic/training requirements: None before entry.
Personality/physical requirements: Minimum age 18; physical fitness and strength; minimum height 1.68m. Good eyesight without glasses and good colour vision; good hearing and balance. Courage and safety consciousness; good teamwork; willingness to work shifts.

POLICE OFFICER
Entry levels: N, G, G+, A, D.
GCSEs normally required: No specific requirements, but 4 GCSEs at grade C or above, including English and maths, may exempt you from the standard entry test.
GCSEs which may be useful: Social sciences.
Other academic/training requirements: Some entrants have A-levels or a degree.
Personality/physical requirements: Minimum age 18.5 (16 for cadets, where available). Minimum height requirements are tending to disappear. Character, health, eyesight and physique must be good. Qualities of leadership, ability to work in a team and accept discipline, willingness to work shifts.

PRISON GOVERNOR
Entry levels: AD.
GCSEs normally required: Good spread of GCSEs at grade C or above, including English.
GCSEs which may be useful: Social sciences.
Other academic/training requirements: Usually A-levels and a degree (subjects like social sciences or psychology are useful).
Personality/physical requirements: Physical fitness, qualities of leadership; understanding of people; good health; stable personality.

PRISON OFFICER

Entry levels: N, G, G+.

GCSEs normally required: No formal entrance requirements.
English preferred. Applicants take aptitude test.

GCSEs which may be useful: social sciences.

Other academic/training requirements: None before entry.

Personality/physical requirements: Minimum age 20. Minimum
height generally 1.67m for men and 1.60m for women. Stable
personality; ability to deal authoritatively but sensitively with
people; good health and physique; liking for teamwork and
discipline.

I'M THINKING ABOUT A CAREER IN HOME ECONOMICS OR THE HOTEL AND CATERING INDUSTRY

CHEF/COOK

Entry levels: N, G, GD.

GCSEs normally required: No specific requirements, but some
GCSEs are usually an advantage, especially for college course.

GCSEs which may be useful: Home economics/food studies, science,
French.

Other academic/training requirements: Either direct entry at 16
(perhaps via Youth Training) or full-time college course first.

Personality/physical requirements: Calm approach to pressure; ability
to withstand hot working conditions; very high standards of
hygiene; flair and imagination; good organising abilities and
qualities of leadership, if aiming to be a chef in a big kitchen.

DOMESTIC STAFF

Entry levels: N, G.

GCSEs normally required: No formal qualifications needed.

GCSEs which may be useful: Home economics/food studies.

Other academic/training requirements: None before entry.

Personality/physical requirements: Fitness and energy; tidy worker;
liking for making things look nice. Often, willing to work
unsocial hours.

FAST FOOD SHOP MANAGER
Entry levels: G+, GD, A, AD.
GCSEs normally required: About 4 GCSEs at grade C or above, subjects preferably to include English and maths.
GCSEs which may be useful: Home economics/food studies, business studies.
Other academic/training requirements: Perhaps a business studies or catering course, after GCSEs or A-levels; some graduate entry.
Personality/physical requirements: Good organisational abilities and staff management skills. Interest in selling.

HOME ECONOMIST
Entry levels: GD, AD.
GCSEs normally required: 3-4 GCSEs at grade C or above, to include English and science.
GCSEs which may be useful: Maths, home economics/food studies.
Other academic/training requirements: Diploma/higher diploma taken after GCSEs/A-level(s); or a degree (science A-levels preferred).
Personality/physical requirements: Good communication skills; self confidence; sympathetic approach to people and their problems. For research work, a meticulous scientific approach.

HOTEL/CATERING MANAGER
Entry levels: GD, AD.
GCSEs normally required: 3-4 GCSEs at grade C or above, to include English (or English subject); maths and science preferred.
GCSEs which may be useful: Home economics/food studies, business studies, French.
Other academic/training requirements: Hotel and catering management diploma/higher diploma either after GCSEs or A-levels; or a degree.
Personality/physical requirements: Good organisational abilities and qualities of leadership. A pleasant and helpful manner with customers.

HOTEL/HOUSEKEEPER
Entry levels: G, G+, GD.
GCSEs normally required: Good general education; 4 GCSEs at grade C or above (including English, maths and science) allow you

to take higher level training.

GCSEs which may be useful: Home economics/food studies, science, art/design, business studies.

Other academic/training requirements: you can start after GCSE and train part-time, or take a full-time course before entering into employment.

Personality/physical requirements: Good organisational abilities; flair for making things look good; interest in furnishings and interior decoration; strong sense of hygiene and cleanliness.

HOTEL RECEPTIONIST

Entry levels: G+, GD.

GCSEs normally required: Usually at least 2 GCSEs at grade C or above; English and maths preferred.

GCSEs which may be useful: Modern languages, business studies, IT/office skills.

Other academic/training requirements: Some type of office training and preferably a specific hotel receptionist course – this can be started after GCSEs.

Personality/physical requirements: Pleasant manner with people; smart appearance; good organisational skills; willingness to work shifts.

KITCHEN ASSISTANT

Entry levels: N, G.

GCSEs normally required: No special requirements.

GCSEs which may be useful: Home economics/food studies.

Other academic/training requirements: None before entry.

Personality/physical requirements: Ability to work quickly and in a team; ability to work in hot atmosphere and put up with standing a lot; strong sense of hygiene and personal cleanliness; tidy worker.

WAITER/WAITRESS

Entry levels: N, G.

GCSEs normally required: No special requirements.

GCSEs which may be useful: Home economics/food studies.

Other academic/training requirements: None before entry.

Personality/physical requirements: Good appearance. Faultless standard of personal cleanliness. Pleasant manner with customers; ability to work quickly under pressure.

See also – *I'M THINKING ABOUT A CAREER IN HEALTH, MEDICINE AND PERSONAL SERVICES* for Dietician

I'M THINKING ABOUT A CAREER IN HEALTH, MEDICINE OR PERSONAL SERVICES

AMBULANCE STAFF
Entry levels: N, G.
GCSEs normally required: For some entry schemes, applicants may need 4 GCSEs, preferably including English, maths and science.
GCSEs which may be useful: See above.
Other academic/training requirements: None before entry, but experience of work with people is usually sought.
Personality/physical requirements: Minimum age 18 (16, where cadet schemes operate); fitness and strength; calm and understanding nature; pleasant and helpful manner with patients. Driving licence for ambulance work.

BEAUTICIAN/BEAUTY THERAPIST
Entry levels: N, G, G+, GD, AD.
GCSEs normally required: Minimum of 3 GCSEs preferred, to include English and preferably science.
GCSEs which may be useful: See above.
Other academic/training requirements: Normally a college course after GCSEs or A-levels.
Personality/physical requirements: Liking for people and pleasant manner; fitness and stamina; ability to use electrical equipment, etc; smart, well-groomed appearance and a high standard of personal hygiene; manual dexterity.

CHIROPODIST
Entry levels: AD.
GCSEs normally required: 5 GCSEs at grade C or above, to include English and double science (or equivalent).
GCSEs which may be useful: See above.

Other academic/training requirements: At least 2 A-levels (sciences preferred) then a full-time training course.

Personality/physical requirements: Liking for work with people, especially children and the elderly; manual dexterity and practical skills; care and patience; interest in self-employment if willing to practise privately.

CHIROPRACTOR

Entry levels: AD.

GCSEs normally required: 5 GCSEs at grade C or above, to include English and double science.

GCSEs which may be useful: See above.

Other academic/training requirements: 3 A-levels (sciences), then a full-time training course. Minimum age 18.

Personality/physical requirements: Sensitive touch; calm and reassuring manner with patients; fitness and stamina; business sense.

DENTAL HYGIENIST

Entry levels: G+, A.

GCSEs normally required: 5 GCSEs at grade C or above, to include English language and science.

GCSEs which may be useful: See above.

Other academic/training requirements: Experience as a dental surgery assistant. Applicants should normally be at least 20.

Personality/physical requirements: Pleasant and reassuring manner; good communication skills; manual dexterity; faultless personal hygiene.

DENTAL SURGERY ASSISTANT

Entry levels: N, G, G+, GD.

GCSEs normally required: No formal entry qualifications, but good general education expected – often 2-4 GCSEs at grade C or above, preferably including English and science.

GCSEs which may be useful: See above.

Other academic/training requirements: None before entry, usually though full-time courses are available in some areas.

Personality/physical requirements: Pleasant and helpful manner; high standards of personal hygiene; manual dexterity, physical fitness.

DENTAL TECHNICIAN
Entry levels: G, G+.
GCSEs normally required: Usually 4 GCSEs at grade C or above, to include English, maths and science. Some scope with 3-4 GCSEs, grades D-E, normally to include English, maths and science.
GCSEs which may be useful: Practical/technical subjects.
Other academic/training requirements: Can start in employment after GCSEs, or first take a full-time course.
Personality/physical requirements: Manual dexterity; precision; technical and scientific aptitude; good colour vision.

DENTIST
Entry levels: AD.
GCSEs normally required: Good spread of GCSEs at grade C or above, to include maths and double science (or equivalent), English language preferred.
GCSEs which may be useful: See above.
Other academic/training requirements: Science A-levels, then dentistry degree.
Personality/physical requirements: Manual dexterity; technical and scientific aptitude; good communication skills and reassuring manner with patients; ability to cope with pressure of work. Business sense if planning to enter private practice.

DIETITIAN
Entry levels: AD.
GCSEs normally required: Minimum of 5 GCSEs at grade C or above, to include English and double science, and preferably maths.
GCSEs which may be useful: Home economics/food studies.
Other academic/training requirements: 2 A-levels (chemistry and another science) – or sometimes BTEC/SKIVE national diploma/certificate in science at a good standard – then a degree (usually dietetics).
Personality/physical requirements: Scientific aptitude; good communication skills; ability to relate to all sorts of people; interest in food and nutrition.

DISPENSING OPTICIAN
Entry levels: G+, GD.
GCSEs normally required: 5 GCSEs at grade C or above, including English, maths and science.
GCSEs which may be useful: Practical subjects.
Other academic/training requirements: You can start work after GCSEs or first take a full-time training course.
Personality/physical requirements: Helpful and reassuring manner; good communication skills; interest in selling; fashion-consciousness.

DOCTOR
Entry levels: AD.
GCSEs normally required: Good spread of GCSEs at grade C or above, to include English, maths and double science. High grades needed as entry is very competitive.
GCSEs which may be useful: See above.
Other academic/training requirements: 3 A-levels in maths/science subjects, then a medical degree.
Personality/physical requirements: Strong scientific interest; calm and reassuring manner with patients; excellent skills of observation; concentration; willingness to work long, unsocial hours.

HAIRDRESSER
Entry levels: N, G.
GCSEs normally required: Good general education – no specific GCSEs.
GCSEs which may be useful: English, art, maths and science.
Other academic/training requirements: College course, apprenticeship or Youth Training in order to qualify.
Personality/physical requirements: Pleasant manner with customers; manual dexterity; eye for shape; interest in fashion; no allergies to chemicals, such as perm lotions, and no skin problems. Suitable appearance; high standards of personal hygiene; stamina and ability to stand all day.

HOSPITAL NURSE
Entry levels: G, G+, A, AD.
GCSEs normally required: Good general education – preferably

5 GCSEs at grade C or above. English and science preferred.
GCSEs which may be useful: Home economics/food studies,
child care.
Other academic/training requirements: Higher qualifications, eg A-
levels, requested by some schools/ colleges. Pre-nursing/pre-health
care courses exist in many colleges.
Personality/physical requirements: Practical nature; common sense;
caring and sympathetic approach; energy; sense of responsibility;
liking for teamwork; often, willingness to work shifts.

HOSPITAL PORTER, OPERATING DEPARTMENT ASSISTANT

Entry levels: N, G.
GCSEs normally required: No formal qualifications needed, but
many applicants have some GCSEs.
GCSEs which may be useful: English, maths, science.
Other academic/training requirements: None before entry, but
experience of work with people is usually sought.
Personality/physical requirements: Minimum age 18; fitness and
strength; calm and understanding nature; pleasant and helpful
manner with patients.

MEDICAL TECHNICAL OFFICER

Entry levels: G+, A, AD.
GCSEs normally required: 4 GCSEs at grade C or above, to include
English, maths and double science.
GCSEs which may be useful: See above.
GCSEs normally required: Few openings with GCSEs. Most entrants
have A-levels (sciences) or Higher National Diploma/degree taken
after A-levels.
Personality/physical requirements: Meticulous attention to detail;
interest in science; liking for laboratory-based work; patience.

NURSING AUXILIARY

Entry levels: N, G.
GCSEs normally required: No specific requirements, although some
health authorities require GCSEs.
GCSEs which may be useful: Home economics/food studies, science,
child care.

Other academic/training requirements: None before entry.
Personality/physical requirements: Minimum age 17/18. Energy;
pleasant and helpful manner with colleagues and patients;
common sense and practical outlook.

OCCUPATIONAL THERAPIST
Entry levels: AD.
GCSEs normally required: Minimum of 5 GCSEs at grade C or
above, to include English and science.
GCSEs which may be useful: Maths, practical subjects.
Other academic/training requirements: 2 A-levels (sciences preferred)
then a full-time degree in occupational therapy.
Personality/physical requirements: Fitness; sympathetic and caring
approach to patients; practical and imaginative attitude to
problem solving; patience and perseverance.

OPHTHALMIC OPTICIAN
Entry levels: AD.
GCSEs normally required: Minimum of 5 GCSEs at grade C or
above, to include English, maths and double science (or
equivalent).
GCSEs which may be useful: See above.
Other academic/training requirements: 2 A-levels (maths and science
subjects) then degree in optometry/ophthalmics.
Personality/physical requirements: Ability to get on well with people
and reassure them. Liking for meticulous work; business sense if
planning to practise privately.

ORTHOPTIST
Entry levels: AD.
GCSEs normally required: Minimum of 5 GCSEs at grade C or
above, to include English, maths and science.
GCSEs which may be useful: See above.
Other academic/training requirements: 2 A-levels (science preferred)
then full-time orthoptics degree.
Personality/physical requirements: Ability to relate well to patients,
especially young children. Good communication skills; ability to
observe accurately and interpret test results; patience.

OSTEOPATH

Entry levels: AD.

GCSEs normally required: For most reputable training schools, 5 GCSEs at grade C or above, to include English and double science.

GCSEs which may be useful: See above.

Other academic/training requirements: 2 A-levels (sciences), then a full-time training course. For training at London College of Osteopathic Medicine, candidates need to be qualified doctors.

Personality/physical requirements: Sensitive touch; calm and reassuring manner with patients; fitness and stamina; business sense.

PHARMACIST

Entry levels: AD.

GCSEs normally required: Good spread of GCSEs at grade C or above, to include English, maths and double science.

GCSEs which may be useful: See above.

Other academic/training requirements: Science A-levels (to include chemistry), then a pharmacy degree.

Personality/physical requirements: Meticulous attention to detail; good organising abilities; good communication skills and helpful manner with customers. Strong sense of responsibility.

PHARMACY TECHNICIAN

Entry levels: G+.

GCSEs normally required: 3 or 4 GCSEs at grade C or above, to include English, maths, science.

GCSEs which may be useful: See above.

Other academic/training requirements: None before entry.

Personality/physical requirements: Attention to detail; strong sense of responsibility; ability to deal helpfully with customers.

PHYSIOLOGICAL MEASUREMENT TECHNICIAN
(eg Cardiology, Audiology etc)

Entry levels: G+, A.

GCSEs normally required: Preferably a minimum of 4 GCSEs at grade C or above, to include English (or English subject), maths and double science.

GCSEs which may be useful: Technical/practical subjects.

Other academic/training requirements: 2 science A-levels, or 4 GCSEs including double science (grade C or above) give entry at higher level.
Personality/physical requirements: Technical abilities; precision; reassuring manner with patients.

PHYSIOTHERAPIST

Entry levels: AD.
GCSEs normally required: Minimum of 5 GCSEs at grade C or above, to include English, maths and double science.
GCSEs which may be useful: See above.
Other academic/training requirements: 2 A-levels (should include a science – preferably biology); then full-time degree in physiotherapy.
Personality/physical requirements: Fitness and stamina; sensitive touch; sympathetic approach to patients; patience and perseverance.

RADIOGRAPHER

Entry levels: AD.
GCSEs normally required: Minimum of 5 GCSEs at grade C or above, to include English, maths and double science.
GCSEs which may be useful: See above.
Other academic/training requirements: 2 A-levels (sciences preferred) then full-time degree at School of Radiography.
Personality/physical requirements: Reasonable fitness; sympathetic and caring approach to patients; scientific/technical understanding; willingness to work shifts for most opportunities.

SPEECH/LANGUAGE THERAPIST

Entry levels: AD.
GCSEs normally required: Minimum of 5 GCSEs at grade C or above, to include English.
GCSEs which may be useful: Maths, modern languages.
Other academic/training requirements: 2 A-levels (science preferred), then a degree.
Personality/physical requirements: Good communication skills; sensitive ear; ability to relate well to patients, especially children and elderly people; patience and perseverance; imagination and enthusiasm.

I'M THINKING ABOUT A CAREER IN OFFICE WORK OR ADMINISTRATION

ADMINISTRATIVE/BUSINESS MANAGEMENT TRAINEE (Health Service, Industry & Commerce)

Entry levels: GD, A, AD.

GCSEs normally required: About 5 or more GCSEs at grade C or above, to include English and maths.

GCSEs which may be useful: modern languages, geography, business studies/economics, science.

Other academic/training requirements: various ways of getting started – business studies course after GCSEs or A-levels, direct entry from A-levels or degree (any subject).

Personality/physical requirements: Good organisational and administrative abilities; clear thought processes and ability to analyse and present information; ability to supervise staff; good written and oral communication skills; smart appearance.

BILINGUAL SECRETARY

Entry levels: GD, AD.

GCSEs normally required: Several GCSEs at grade C or above, to include English and a modern language (2 are preferred).

GCSEs which may be useful: Business studies, IT, office skills, geography, maths.

Other academic/training requirements: A-level in at least 1 modern language required for higher level courses; bilingual secretarial course to be taken after GCSEs, A-levels (the usual entry point) or a degree.

Personality/physical requirements: Good written and oral communication skills; attention to detail; high standards of accuracy and presentation; smart appearance.

CIVIL SERVICE ADMINISTRATIVE ASSISTANT/ OFFICER

Entry levels: G+.

GCSEs normally required: 2 GCSEs at grade C or above, to include English, for Assistant level; 5 GCSEs at grade C or above, to include English, for Officer level.

GCSEs which may be useful: Maths, social sciences; subjects such as modern languages, history, geography, business studies.
Other academic/training requirements: None before entry.
Personality/physical requirements: Good organisational abilities; high standards of accuracy and attention to detail; capable of working under pressure for some jobs; ability to deal with the public.

COMPANY SECRETARY

Entry levels: A, AD.
GCSEs normally required: 5 GCSEs at grade C or above, to include English and preferably maths.
GCSEs which may be useful: Business studies/economics.
Other academic/training requirements: 2 A-levels or BTEC/SKIVE National/Certificate, and often a degree.
Personality/physical requirements: Very good organisational and administrative abilities; high level of written and oral communication skills; attention to detail; self confidence.

CLERK/CLERICAL ASSISTANT

Entry levels: G, G+.
GCSEs normally required: Good general education – higher grade GCSEs are often sought by employers. English and maths preferred.
GCSEs which may be useful: Office skills, IT.
Other academic/training requirements: Perhaps an office training course before starting a job.
Personality/physical requirements: Well organised approach to work; accuracy and attention to detail; tidy worker; ability to deal with public/customers in some jobs.

ENVIRONMENTAL HEALTH OFFICER

Entry levels: AD.
GCSEs normally required: 5 GCSEs at grade C or above, to include English, maths and double science.
GCSEs which may be useful: Practical and technical subjects.
Other academic/training requirements: A-levels (at least 1 science), then a diploma or degree in environmental health.
Personality/physical requirements: Good powers of observation and attention for detail; self confidence and confident manner with people; good written and oral communication skills.

EXECUTIVE OFFICER (Civil Service)

Entry levels: A, AD.

GCSEs normally required: About 5 GCSEs at grade C or above, to include English and preferably maths.

GCSEs which may be useful: Modern languages, history, geography, business studies.

Other academic/training requirements: Normally 2 A -levels (or equivalent), but many recruits are graduates.

Personality/physical requirements: good organisational and administrative abilities; good written and oral communication skills; ability to deal with and supervise people; attention to detail.

HEALTH AND SAFETY INSPECTOR

Entry levels: AD.

GCSEs normally required: Good spread of GCSEs at grade C or above, to include maths. English and science preferred.

GCSEs which may be useful: Practical and technical subjects.

Other academic/training requirements: A-levels (often sciences), followed by a degree or Higher National Diploma in a scientific or technological subject.

Personality/physical requirements: Practical approach and common sense; safety awareness; technical/mechanical aptitudes; good communication skills, including ability to speak well in public situations; powers of persuasion.

LOCAL AUTHORITY ADMINISTRATOR

Entry levels: G+, GD, A, AD.

GCSEs normally required: 3 GCSEs at grade C or above, to include English and preferably maths.

GCSEs which may be useful: Business studies, IT.

Other academic/training requirements: Various levels of entry. You may be able to start with GCSEs or A-levels, but a diploma or degree taken after GCSEs or A-levels may offer advantages.

Personality/physical requirements: Good organisational and administrative abilities; written and oral communication skills; clear thought processes; able to present information clearly; able to deal with people and supervise staff.

LOCAL AUTHORITY CLERK

Entry levels: G+.
GCSEs normally required: 3 or more GCSEs at grade C or above, preferably to include English and maths.
GCSEs which may be useful: Business studies, IT.
Other academic/training requirements: None before entry.
Personality/physical requirements: Attention to detail; accuracy; tidy worker; well organised approach; good communication skills (written and oral); ability to deal with public in some posts; teamwork.

PERSONNEL OFFICER

Entry levels: A, AD.
GCSEs normally required: 5 GCSEs at grade C or above, to include English and maths.
GCSEs which may be useful: Business studies/economics; any academic subjects.
Other academic/training requirements: 2 A-levels and often a degree.
Personality/physical requirements: Good organisational and administrative abilities; good interpersonal skills; high standards of written and oral communication skills.

POSTAL EXECUTIVE

Entry levels: AD.
GCSEs normally required: 5 GCSEs at grade C or above, to include English and preferably maths.
GCSEs which may be useful: Business studies, design and technology, IT.
Other academic/training requirements: A-levels (or equivalent), followed by a degree (or BTEC higher national/certificate in case of IT specialism).
Personality/physical requirements: Good organisational and administrative abilities; good written and oral communication skills; ability to deal with and supervise people; attention to detail.

RECEPTIONIST

Entry levels: G, G+, GD.
GCSEs normally required: Good general education – higher grade GCSEs are an advantage. English often required.

GCSEs which may be useful: Maths, modern languages, office skills, IT.

Other academic/training requirements: An office training course or receptionist course is often an advantage.

Personality/physical requirements: Smart appearance and pleasant and helpful manner; ability to deal with awkward visitors and to cope under pressure.

SECRETARY/PERSONAL ASSISTANT

Entry levels: N, G, G+, GD, AD.

GCSEs normally required: 4 GCSEs, including English, although it is possible to achieve promotion from lower levels of entry.

GCSEs which may be useful: Maths, modern languages, office skills, business studies, IT.

Other academic/training requirements: A secretarial course taken after GCSEs or A-levels. Higher qualifications often lead to better jobs.

Personality/physical requirements: Calm and capable manner; accurate and quick worker; good at spelling and grammar; good organisational abilities; smart appearance; versatility.

SPECIALIST SECRETARY (Medical, Legal, Agricultural)

Entry levels: GD, AD.

GCSEs normally required: About 4 GCSEs at grade C or above, to include English. Maths preferred.

GCSEs which may be useful: IT, business studies.

Other academic/training requirements: Secretarial course (preferably a specialist course) taken after GCSEs or perhaps A-levels.

Personality/physical requirements: Interest in area of specialism; high level of secretarial skills and meticulous standards of accuracy and presentation; calm and capable manner; good organisational abilities; versatility; smart appearance.

TAX INSPECTOR

Entry levels: AD.

GCSEs normally required: Good spread of GCSEs at grade C or above. English and maths preferred.

GCSEs which may be useful: See above.

Other academic/training requirements: A-levels and degree.

Personality/physical requirements: Clear thought processes and powers of analysis; good written and oral communication skills; good organisational and administrative abilities; high level of numeracy; self confidence.

TELEPHONIST

Entry levels: G, G+.
GCSEs normally required: Good general education; higher grade GCSEs may be preferred, especially in English.
GCSEs which may be useful: IT, modern languages.
Other academic/training requirements: None before entry essential, but an office training course may be an advantage.
Personality/physical requirements: Pleasant speaking voice; calm and helpful manner; ability to cope with pressure and awkward callers; liking for sedentary job.

TRADING STANDARDS OFFICER

Entry levels: A, AD.
GCSEs normally required: 3 GCSEs at grade C or above, to include English, maths and science.
GCSEs which may be useful: Business studies, design and technology, home economics/food studies.
Other academic/training requirements: A-levels (sciences may be preferred) or equivalent. Often graduate entry.
Personality/physical requirements: Meticulous attention to detail and accuracy; good written and oral communication skills; practical and technical abilities; self confidence.

TYPIST/WORD PROCESSOR OPERATOR

Entry levels: G, G+, GD.
GCSEs normally required: Good general education, higher grade GCSEs may be preferred. English and maths preferred.
GCSEs which may be useful: IT, office skills.
Other academic/training requirements: Ability to type is usually expected before starting a job – you could learn to type at school or college.
Personality/physical requirements: Accuracy; good spelling and grammar; ability to concentrate and work quickly; confidence with electronic equipment; liking for sedentary job.

I'M THINKING ABOUT A CAREER IN COMPUTING

APPLICATIONS PROGRAMMER

Entry levels: G+, GD, A, AD.

GCSEs normally required: about 5 GCSEs at grade C or above, with English, maths and science subjects.

GCSEs which may be useful: IT, electronics/design and technology.

GCSEs normally required: in most cases, at least 1 A-level and often a diploma or degree following A-levels, but still some openings at lower level for those performing well in aptitude tests.

Personality/physical requirements: meticulous attention to detail; ability to concentrate; clear thought processes; powers of logic and analysis.

COMPUTER SERVICE TECHNICIAN

Entry levels: G+, A, AD

GCSEs normally required: Usually 4-5 GCSEs at grade C or above, preferably to include English and maths.

GCSEs which may be useful: IT.

Other academic/training requirements: Most entrants have BTEC/SKIVE awards at national or higher national level in eg computer studies, if not degree

Personality/physical requirements: Ability to concentrate and pay attention to detail; systematic approach, but with ability to work quickly.

MICROELECTRONICS ENGINEER

Entry levels: AD.

GCSEs normally required: Good spread of GCSEs at grade C or above, to include English, maths and science.

GCSEs which may be useful: Design and technology/engineering subjects, electronics.

Other academic/training requirements: A-levels (maths/physics or computer science), then a degree in electronic engineering or related subject.

Personality/physical requirements: Technical/design abilities; logical mind; inventiveness; perseverance and attention to detail.

SYSTEMS ANALYST

Entry levels: AD.
GCSEs normally required: Good spread of GCSEs at grade C or above, to include English and maths.
GCSEs which may be useful: Business studies, IT.
Other academic/training requirements: A-levels and usually a degree (not necessarily in relevant subject) or BTEC/SKIVE higher national award.
Personality/physical requirements: Analytical and creative mind; good communication skills (oral and written); ability to relate to people; attention to detail.

SYSTEMS PROGRAMMER/SOFTWARE ENGINEER

Entry levels: A, AD.
GCSEs normally required: Good spread of GCSEs at grade C or above, to include English, maths and science.
GCSEs which may be useful: Design and technology/engineering subjects, electronics.
Other academic/training requirements: A-levels (including maths or science). Many companies prefer a degree in maths, computer science or electronic engineering. BTEC/SKIVE higher national awards also available.
Personality/physical requirements: Technical and mathematical skills; problem solving abilities; perseverance and attention to detail; ability to work well in a team.

I'M THINKING ABOUT A CAREER IN ENGINEERING

CHARTERED ENGINEER

Entry levels: AD.
GCSEs normally required: 5 GCSEs at grade C or above, to include maths, science and preferably English.
GCSEs which may be useful: Design and technology, technical and practical subjects, IT, modern languages.
Other academic/training requirements: Maths/science (especially physics) A-levels (or BTEC/SKIVE equivalent), degree in engineering.

Personality/physical requirements: Creativity and initiative; practical approach to problem solving; logic and analytical abilities; good written and oral communication skills; ability to mix with all sorts of people and supervise staff.

ELECTRICIAN

Entry levels: G.

GCSEs normally required: Usually a few GCSEs at least at grade E or above, with preferred subjects being maths, science, design and technology, practical and technical subjects.

GCSEs which may be useful: See above.

Other academic/training requirements: None before entry which is usually via an apprenticeship or Youth Training.

Personality/physical requirements: Ability to concentrate on details; manual dexterity; good colour vision; for some jobs, ability to deal with public or customers.

ENGINEERING CRAFTSMAN/WOMAN

Entry levels: G.

GCSEs normally required: Reasonable GCSEs (say, grade E or above) in maths, science and English.

GCSEs which may be useful: Design and technology, practical and technical subjects.

Other academic/training requirements: Entry through apprenticeship/Youth Training.

Personality/physical requirements: Manual dexterity – good hands and with machinery; ability to work accurately and with attention to detail; liking for teamwork.

ENGINEERING OPERATIVE

Entry levels: N, G.

GCSEs normally required: No formal qualifications, but good general education preferred, especially in English, maths, practical and technical subjects.

GCSEs which may be useful: Science.

Other academic/training requirements: None before entry.

Personality/physical requirements: Liking for teamwork; good with hands and machinery; ability to concentrate; safety consciousness.

ENGINEERING TECHNICIAN

Entry levels: G+, GD.

GCSEs normally required: Usually 3-4 GCSEs at grade C or above in subjects such as maths, English, science, design and technology, practical subjects. Some possibility of entry with slightly lower qualifications.

GCSEs which may be useful: See above.

Other academic/training requirements: Entry through technician apprenticeship or college course such as BTEC/SKIVE National Diploma.

Personality/physical requirements: Technical skills; ability to understand engineering theory, drawings etc; manual dexterity; attention to fine detail; good communication skills; initiative.

INCORPORATED ENGINEER

Entry levels: AD.

GCSEs normally required: 5 GCSEs at grade C or above, to include English, maths, science.

GCSEs which may be useful: Design and technology, technical and practical subjects, IT, modern languages.

Other academic/training requirements: maths/science (especially physics) A-levels (or BTEC/SKIVE equivalent), plus BTEC/SKIVE Higher National Diploma/part-time Higher National Certificate or degree in engineering.

Personality/physical requirements: Creativity and initiative; practical approach to problem solving; logic and analytical abilities; good written and oral communication skills; ability to mix with all sorts of people and supervise staff.

MOTOR MECHANIC

Entry levels: N, G.

GCSEs normally required: GCSEs at grade C or above often asked for, with preferred subjects being English, maths and science, practical subjects.

GCSEs which may be useful: See above.

Other academic/training requirements: None before entry, which is usually via an apprenticeship or Youth Training. Some college courses exist.

Personality/physical requirements: Skills in working with hands and machinery; reasonable fitness; safety consciousness; sense of responsibility; attention to detail; careful and tidy worker; liking for teamwork.

SHEET METAL WORKER/WELDER

Entry levels: N, G.
GCSEs normally required: GCSEs at grade D or above in at least English, maths and science preferred.
GCSEs which may be useful: Technical/practical subjects.
Other academic/training requirements: none before entry.
Personality/physical requirements: reasonable fitness; skills in working with hands and machinery; safety consciousness; careful and tidy worker.

I'M THINKING ABOUT A CAREER WORKING WITH CHILDREN OR YOUNG PEOPLE

CARE ASSISTANT

Entry levels: N, G, G+, GD.
GCSEs normally required: No specific requirements, but a good general education is usually expected, with higher grade GCSEs being advantageous.
GCSEs which may be useful: Child care, home economics, English, social sciences.
Other academic/training requirements: Perhaps a 'care' or social work course, or YT.
Personality/physical requirements: Plenty of energy; ability to keep children under control; sympathetic nature; sense of responsibility.

CAREERS OFFICER

Entry levels: AD.
GCSEs normally required: 5 GCSEs at grade C or above, usually including English.
GCSEs which may be useful: Social sciences.
Other academic/training requirements: A-levels and degree, or approved diploma. Experience in other work situations is advantageous.

Personality/physical requirements: Real understanding of young people; interest in psychology; good communication skills, especially listening and analysing; ability to relate to all kinds of people; retentive memory.

EDUCATIONAL PSYCHOLOGIST

Entry levels: AD.
GCSEs normally required: Good spread of GCSEs at grade C or above, to include maths and preferably English.
GCSEs which may be useful: Science, social sciences; statistics.
Other academic/training requirements: A-levels, then psychology degree and teaching requirements.
Personality/physical requirements: Good powers of observation; analytical mind; good communication and interpersonal skills – ability to inspire children's trust.

NURSERY NURSE

Entry levels: GD, A.
GCSEs normally required: Usually at least 2-3 GCSEs at grade C or above, preferably to include English.
GCSEs which may be useful: Home economics, child care, music, crafts, science, social sciences.
Other academic/training requirements: NNEB course after GCSEs – or even A-levels.
Personality/physical requirements: Cheerful but firm manner; plenty of energy and imagination; sense of responsibility and safety consciousness; well-organised approach.

RESIDENTIAL SOCIAL WORKER

Entry levels: AD.
GCSEs normally required: 4-5 GCSEs at grade C or above, including English.
GCSEs which may be useful: Social sciences.
Other academic/training requirements: Diploma in Social Work, after A-levels or equivalent.
Personality/physical requirements: Ability to relate well with wide range of people; good communication skills,; ability to handle stress.

TEACHER

Entry levels: AD.

GCSEs normally required: Minimum of 3 GCSEs at grade C or above, to include English and maths. Other subjects will depend on age range/specialism.

GCSEs which may be useful: See above.

Other academic/training requirements: A-levels, then degree and teacher training, or BEd degree.

Personality/physical requirements: Excellent communication skills, especially oral; ability to relate to children and motivate them; good organisational abilities; stamina; self confidence and patience. Other requirements depend upon age range/specialism.

YOUTH AND COMMUNITY WORKER

Entry levels: AD.

GCSEs normally required: 5 GCSEs at grade C or above, usually to include English.

GCSEs which may be useful: Social sciences.

Other academic/training requirements: Usually A-levels, then diploma or degree.

Personality/physical requirements: Good organisational abilities; excellent communication and interpersonal skills; ability to motivate young people without over-intruding; firm manner; energy and patience. Specialist skills or interests, eg in sport, can be useful.

See also – *I'M THINKING ABOUT A CAREER IN THE SOCIAL SERVICES* for Probation Officer, Social Worker etc.

See also – *I'M THINKING ABOUT A CAREER IN HEALTH OR MEDICINE* for Doctor, Speech Therapist, Orthoptist etc.

I'M THINKING ABOUT A CAREER IN SOCIAL & COMMUNITY SERVICES

CHARITIES MANAGER/ORGANISER

Entry levels: A, AD.

GCSEs normally required: About 5 GCSEs at grade C or above.

English is preferred.

GCSEs which may be useful: Maths, business studies, social sciences.

Other academic/training requirements: A-levels and often a degree. Perhaps a social work training or similar experience.

Personality/physical requirements: Excellent organising abilities; persuasiveness; interest in fund-raising; good communication skills – ability to motivate people; drive and energy.

HEALTH VISITOR

Entry levels: G+, A, AD.

GCSEs normally required: Minimum of 5 GCSEs at grade C or above, preferably to include English, maths and science.

GCSEs which may be useful: Home economics/food studies, social sciences, child care.

Other academic/training requirements: Nurse training then health visitor's course. A-levels may be an advantage.

Personality/physical requirements: Friendly and approachable manner; good powers of observation; good organisational abilities; strong sense of responsibility; good communication skills (written and oral); often, ability to drive.

PROBATION OFFICER

Entry levels: AD.

GCSEs normally required: 5 GCSEs at grade C or above, preferably to include English and maths.

GCSEs which may be useful: Social sciences, statistics.

Other academic/training requirements: Diploma in social work, after A-levels.

Personality/physical requirements: Approachable manner but firm when necessary; good communication and interpersonal skills – ability to get on with all types of people; insight and maturity.

PSYCHOLOGIST/PSYCHOTHERAPIST

Entry levels: AD.

GCSEs normally required: 5 GCSEs at grade C or above, to include maths and preferably English.

GCSEs which may be useful: Science, social sciences, statistics.

Other academic/training requirements: A-levels, then degree.

Personality/physical requirements: Strong powers of observation and analysis; ability to inspire trust in others; good communication skills, especially listening; self confidence; insight and maturity.

RELIGIOUS MINISTRY (Priest, Minister etc)

Entry levels: G, G+, A, AD.

GCSEs normally required: Requirements vary from one denomination to another and entry without qualifications is possible – usually, however, a good spread of GCSEs at grade C or above is welcomed.

GCSEs which may be useful: English, religious studies, history.

Other academic/training requirements: Often A-levels and a degree; theological training.

Personality/physical requirements: Commitment and faith are vital; good communication and interpersonal skills; approachable and caring manner; energy and drive; ability to motivate others and inspire confidence.

RESIDENTIAL CARE ASSISTANT

(eg Homes for Elderly)

Entry levels: N, G, G+, GD.

GCSEs normally required: No specific requirements but good general education preferred. GCSEs at grade C or above can enable you to become qualified.

GCSEs which may be useful: English, home economics, social sciences.

Other academic/training requirements: Perhaps a college course in a 'care' subject or pre-social work.

Personality/physical requirements: Good organisational abilities; sympathetic and pleasant manner, but capable of being firm when necessary; willingness to work unsocial hours (not necessarily resident).

SOCIAL WORKER

Entry levels: AD.

GCSEs normally required: 5 GCSEs at grade C or above, preferably to include English and maths.

GCSEs which may be useful: Statistics, social sciences.

Other academic/training requirements: Diploma in social work, after A-levels.

Personality/physical requirements: Real interest in people combined with ability not to get over-involved in cases; good powers of observation; good communication skills (written and oral); power of persuasion; strong sense of responsibility; maturity.

See also – *I'M THINKING ABOUT A CAREER WORKING WITH CHILDREN OR YOUNG PEOPLE* for Residential Social Worker and Youth & Community Worker

I'M THINKING ABOUT A CAREER IN FINANCE

ACCOUNTANT (Chartered, Certified, Management, Public Service)
Entry levels: GD, A, AD.
GCSEs normally required: At least 5 GCSEs at grade C or above, to include maths and English.
GCSEs which may be useful: Business studies/economics, modern languages.
Other academic/training requirements: Entry usually after A-levels or equivalent, or degree (any subject).
Personality/physical requirements: Attention to detail; good communication skills (oral and written) and interpersonal skills; sound judgment; ability to present a case; smart appearance; honesty and integrity.

ACCOUNTING TECHNICIAN
Entry levels: G, G+.
GCSEs normally required: GCSEs, to include English and maths, an advantage.
GCSEs which may be useful: Business studies/economics, IT.
Other academic/training requirements: None before entry.
Personality/physical requirements: Attention to detail; ability to concentrate and cope with generally sedentary work; neat worker.

ACTUARY
Entry levels: A, AD.
GCSEs normally required: At least 5 GCSEs at grade C or above,

including English and maths.

GCSEs which may be useful: Statistics, business studies/economics.

Other academic/training requirements: A-levels including maths and almost always a degree.

Personality/physical requirements: Strong mathematical abilities; attention to detail and methodical approach; good communication skills (oral, written, numerical); sound judgment.

BANK CLERK, BUILDING SOCIETY CLERK, INSURANCE CLERK

Entry levels: G, G+.

GCSEs normally required: At least some GCSEs at grade C or above, to include English and preferably maths. In some areas, lower grade GCSEs may be sufficient.

GCSEs which may be useful: Modern languages, business studies/economics, IT.

Other academic/training requirements: None before entry.

Personality/physical requirements: Good powers of concentration and attention to detail; pleasant and helpful manner when dealing with customers; absolute honesty and discretion; smart appearance.

BANKER/BANK MANAGER/BUILDING SOCIETY MANAGER

Entry levels: G+, A, AD.

GCSEs normally required: Good spread of GCSEs at grade C or above, to include English and preferably maths.

GCSEs which may be useful: Modern languages, business studies/economics, IT.

Other academic/training requirements: Entry possible after A-levels or degree (any subject).

Personality/physical requirements: Managerial potential – good organisational abilities; honesty and trust; ability to motivate staff and inspire trust in others; good communication/negotiating skills; sound judgment; smart appearance; often, willingness to move to gain promotion.

INSURANCE BROKER/UNDERWRITER

Entry levels: G+, GD, A, AD.

GCSEs normally required: At least 4 GCSEs at grade C or above, to include English and maths.

GCSEs which may be useful: Business studies/economics.

Other academic/training requirements: Entry possible after GCSEs, BTEC National Diploma, A-levels or degree.

Personality/physical requirements: Methodical approach and attention to detail; sound judgment; good communication skills (written and oral); honesty and integrity.

INSURANCE SALESMAN/SALESWOMAN

Entry levels: G+.

GCSEs normally required: About 4 GCSEs at grade C or above, including English and maths.

GCSEs which may be useful: Business studies/economics.

Other academic/training requirements: None before entry but there may be minimum age limits.

Personality/physical requirements: Easy and confident manner with all kinds of people; honesty, discretion and attention; often, a willingness to work unsocial hours; good organisational abilities; often, ability to drive; smart appearance.

INVESTMENT ANALYST

Entry levels: AD.

GCSEs normally required: 5 GCSEs at grade C or above, including English and maths.

GCSEs which may be useful: Statistics, business studies/economics.

Other academic/training requirements: Usually A-levels and degree (sometimes in specialist area).

Personality/physical requirements: Ability to analyse and interpret information; good oral and written communication skills; self confidence and sound judgment; strong interest in economics.

STOCKBROKER

Entry levels: G+, A, AD.

GCSEs normally required: No set qualifications, but normally at least 5 GCSEs at grade C or above, including English and maths.

GCSEs which may be useful: Business studies/economics, IT, modern languages, geography, science.

Other academic/training requirements: Most entrants have A-levels or a degree (any subject).

Personality/physical requirements: Ability to analyse information; ability to work under considerable pressure; sound judgment and financial sense; good communication and negotiating skills.

I'M THINKING ABOUT A CAREER IN ART AND DESIGN

ART TEACHER
Entry levels: AD.
GCSEs normally required: 5 GCSEs at grade C or above, including English, maths and preferably art.
GCSEs which may be useful: Design and technology.
Other academic/training requirements: A-levels (possibly followed by Foundation Art course), then BEd or art degree plus postgraduate teacher training.
Personality/physical requirements: Real interest in teaching; firm manner when necessary; good organisational abilities and excellent communication skills; energy.

ARTIST
Entry levels: GD, AD.
GCSEs normally required: Although talent is the main thing (and it is possible to be an artist without qualifications), most artists do take a formal art training for which 3-5 GCSEs at grade C or above may be needed.
GCSEs which may be useful: Art, any craft subjects.
Other academic/training requirements: Usually art training started after GCSE or A-levels.
Personality/physical requirements: Real talent and creativity.

DESIGNER (Fashion, Furniture, Interior etc)
Entry levels: GD, AD.
GCSEs normally required: Usually at least 3 and preferably 5 GCSEs at grade C or above. Art portfolio more important than particular subjects.
GCSEs which may be useful: Art/design, English, subject appropriate to specialism – eg crafts, textiles/dress etc.

Other academic/training requirements: Various courses – eg BTEC Diploma or degree in art and design after Foundation Course and/or A-levels.

Personality/physical requirements: Creativity and imagination; real talent; strong visual sense; practical attitudes; good communication skills; ability to work under pressure; often, business sense.

DISPLAY DRESSER

Entry levels: N, G, G+.

GCSEs normally required: No particular GCSEs but this is a competitive job, so a few higher grade GCSEs may help.

GCSEs which may be useful: Art, practical/craft subjects.

Other academic/training requirements: None before entry, usually, but perhaps an art or design course.

Personality/physical requirements: Reasonable fitness; quick and tidy workmanship; good eye for design and colouring; imagination.

FLORIST

Entry levels: G, G+.

GCSEs normally required: Good general education – 3 GCSEs at grade C or above, to include English, maths and science for some routes.

GCSEs which may be useful: Science, art/design, practical subjects.

Other academic/training requirements: Usually apprenticeship/ Youth Training.

Personality/physical requirements: Quick, careful worker; artistic/design flair; colour sense and eye for shape; good with people if working with customers.

GRAPHIC DESIGNER/ILLUSTRATOR

Entry levels: GD, AD.

GCSEs normally required: 4-5 GCSEs at grade C or above, including English and science. Some entry without formal qualifications.

GCSEs which may be useful: Design and technology, art.

Other academic/training requirements: specialist training either after GCSEs or Foundation Course and/or A-levels.

Personality/physical requirements: Technical aptitude and

understanding; meticulous attention to detail; care and precision; draughtsmanship skills rather than creativity.

MUSEUM/ART GALLERY CURATOR
Entry levels: AD.
GCSEs normally required: Good spread of GCSEs at grade C or above, including English and preferably art and modern languages.
GCSEs which may be useful: Classical and/or modern languages, history, design and technology, textiles, science for specialist collections.
Other academic/training requirements: Usually a degree (often in a relevant subject, such as fine art or art history), after A-levels. Many entrants have postgraduate qualifications or research experience.
Personality/physical requirements: Scholarly mind; excellent aesthetic judgment; good organisational abilities and communication skills (oral and written); wide-ranging interests.

PHOTOGRAPHER
Entry levels: G, G+, A, AD.
GCSEs normally required: no specific requirements, but if you want to train formally, a good general education up to about 4 GCSEs at grade C or above, depending on the course.
GCSEs which may be useful: English, science or maths, art, photography.
Other academic/training requirements: Training courses are available after GCSEs or A-levels.
Personality/physical requirements: Good eyesight and colour vision; imagination; patience and care; aptitude for using technical equipment; good oral communication skills and ability to get on with people.

PRESS PHOTOGRAPHER
Entry levels: G+, AD.
GCSEs normally required: 5 GCSEs at grade C or above, preferably including English.
GCSEs which may be useful: Art, photography; sciences.
Other academic/training requirements: Entry is either after GCSEs or following pre-entry course for holders of 1 A-level. Some entrants

have no formal training, but they are older people.
Personality/physical requirements: Care and patience; persistent
manner; technical aptitude; ability to persuade people when
necessary; fitness and stamina; willingness to work unsocial hours.

I'M THINKING ABOUT A CAREER IN INFORMATION OR IN A CULTURAL PROFESSION

ARCHAEOLOGIST
Entry levels: AD.
GCSEs normally required: Good spread of GCSEs at grade C or
above.
GCSEs which may be useful: English, history, classical languages,
science.
Other academic/training requirements: A-levels, then a degree.
Personality/physical requirements: Precision and attention to detail;
patience; scholarly approach, yet imaginative and practical; good
organisational abilities and communication skills; manual
dexterity and strong observational power.

ARCHIVIST
Entry levels: AD.
GCSEs normally required: Good spread of GCSEs at grade C or
above, to include English.
GCSEs which may be useful: Modern and classical languages, history.
Other academic/training requirements: A-levels, then a degree.
Personality/physical requirements: Attention to detail; patience and
care; enquiring mind; good organisational abilities; sound
judgment; good communication skills; wide-ranging interests.

AUTHOR
Entry levels: N, G, G+, A, AD.
GCSEs normally required: No formal qualifications needed – but
most authors are well qualified academically.
GCSEs which may be useful: English, IT.
Other academic/training requirements: None.

Personality/physical requirements: Real talent; drive and persistence; self discipline and ability to concentrate; imagination and creativity.

INTERPRETER/TRANSLATOR

Entry levels: AD.
GCSEs normally required: Good spread of GCSEs at grade C or above, to include English, a modern language (preferably 2).
GCSEs which may be useful: Most subjects; classical languages.
Other academic/training requirements: language degree.
Personality/physical requirements: Real fluency in foreign language (preferably more than 1); excellent communication skills; attention to detail and accuracy; ability to concentrate and work well under considerable pressure; good hearing, for interpreter.

JOURNALIST

Entry levels: G+, A, AD.
GCSEs normally required: 5 GCSEs at grade C or above, including English.
GCSEs which may be useful: IT; most other subjects.
Other academic/training requirements: Entry after GCSEs, A-levels or pre-entry course or degree (both these last 2 require A-levels).
Personality/physical requirements: energy and stamina; curiosity and persistence; accuracy; good communication skills (written, listening); ability to work well under pressure; willingness to work unsocial hours.

LIBRARIAN/INFORMATION OFFICER

Entry levels: AD.
GCSEs normally required: Good spread of GCSEs at grade C or above, to include English. Maths and modern language preferred.
GCSEs which may be useful: IT. Science for specialist/industrial librarianship.
Other academic/training requirements: A-levels then degree.
Personality/physical requirements: Enquiring mind and retentive memory; good communication skills (oral and written); interest in seeking out information; ability to deal with all types of people in a helpful way; good organisational skills; analytical approach to problems.

LIBRARY ASSISTANT/INFORMATION ASSISTANT

Entry levels: G+, GD.

GCSEs normally required: 4-5 GCSEs at grade C or above, including English and preferably maths.

GCSEs which may be useful: IT.

Other academic/training requirements: Entry either after GCSEs or full-time BTEC National Diploma. Information Assistants commonly require A-levels.

Personality/physical requirements: Reasonable fitness; good communication skills and ability to deal with all sorts of people; enquiring mind and retentive memory; usually, willingness to work shift and unsocial hours.

MUSEUM ASSISTANT

Entry levels: G+, A.

GCSEs normally required: at least 4 GCSEs at grade C or above, to include English.

GCSEs which may be useful: History, art/design subjects.

Other academic/training requirements: A-levels or even a degree may be advantageous.

Personality/physical requirements: Careful and tidy workmanship; helpful manner with people; ability to construct displays can be useful; versatility.

MUSEUM CONSERVATION TECHNICIAN

Entry levels: G+, A, AD.

GCSEs normally required: At least 2 GCSEs at grade C or above, to include English.

GCSEs which may be useful: Science, history; craft subjects.

Other academic/training requirements: A-levels or a degree may be needed, though courses are also available after GCSEs in specialist aspects of conservation.

Personality/physical requirements: Accuracy and precision; manual dexterity; patience and good concentration.

PUBLICITY OFFICER/PUBLIC RELATIONS OFFICER

Entry levels: AD.

GCSEs normally required: Good spread of GCSEs, including English.

GCSEs which may be useful: Most subjects.

Other academic/training requirements: A-levels and a degree; perhaps training in journalism.

Personality/physical requirements: Excellent communication skills; good organisational abilities; self confidence; attention to detail and accuracy; creativity; versatility.

PUBLISHER/EDITOR

Entry levels: A, AD.

GCSEs normally required: Good spread of GCSEs at grade C or above, including English.

GCSEs which may be useful: Maths, design subjects, appropriate subjects for specialist publishing, eg languages, science.

Other academic/training requirements: A-levels and usually diploma or degree. Most entrants are graduates.

Personality/physical requirements: Business sense and sound judgment; excellent written and oral communication skills; ability to work well under pressure; creativity; good organisational abilities.

See also – *I'M THINKING ABOUT A CAREER IN SCIENCE* for Information Scientist and Technical Writer.

See also – *I'M THINKING ABOUT A CAREER IN ART & DESIGN* for Museum/Art Gallery Curator

See also – *I'M THINKING ABOUT A CAREER IN SELLING, MARKETING OR ADVERTISING* for Advertising Copywriter.

I'M THINKING ABOUT A CAREER IN SELLING, MARKETING OR ADVERTISING

ADVERTISING ACCOUNT EXECUTIVE
Entry levels: A, AD.
GCSEs normally required: Good spread of GCSEs at grade C or above, to include English and preferably maths.
GCSEs which may be useful: Art/design subjects, social sciences, business studies/economics.
Other academic/training requirements: A-levels and often a degree (any subject).
Personality/physical requirements: Self confidence and good communication skills; diplomacy and good interpersonal skills; energy and self-motivation; good organisational abilities; smart appearance.

ADVERTISING COPYWRITER
Entry levels: A, AD.
GCSEs normally required: 5 GCSEs at grade C or above, to include English.
GCSEs which may be useful: Art/design subjects, social sciences.
Other academic/training requirements: 2 A-levels and usually a diploma or degree (some specialist courses are available).
Personality/physical requirements: Creativity and imagination; ability to work to deadlines and under pressure; flair for using words; liking for teamwork; interest in human behaviour.

ESTATE AGENT/AUCTIONEER
Entry levels: G+, A, AD.
GCSEs normally required: 4-5 GCSEs at grade C or above, to include English and maths.
GCSEs which may be useful: Science, business studies/ economics.
Other academic/training requirements: Entry is possible after GCSEs, A-levels or post-A level diploma or degree.
Personality/physical requirements: Extrovert personality; specialist interest for certain types of auctioneer (eg fine arts); self confidence; good business sense; good judgment.

MARKET RESEARCH INTERVIEWER
Entry levels: G, G+.
GCSEs normally required: No specific requirements – some GCSEs at grade C or above may be preferred, especially in English and perhaps maths.
GCSEs which may be useful: See above.
Other academic/training requirements: None before entry.
Personality/physical requirements: Pleasant voice and warm manner; ability to get on with all sorts of people; self confidence; smart appearance; sometimes ability to drive. Preference for applicants aged at least 18.

MARKETING MANAGER
Entry levels: AD.
GCSEs normally required: 4 GCSEs at grade C or above, to include English and maths.
GCSEs which may be useful: Business studies/economics, modern languages, social sciences.
Other academic/training requirements: Usually A-levels (or equivalent), then a Higher National Diploma or degree (a business studies/marketing degree may be preferred).
Personality/physical requirements: Excellent communication skills (oral, written and negotiating); organisational skills; liking for teamwork; broad interests, including interest in human behaviour.

MARKETING RESEARCH EXECUTIVE
Entry levels: A, AD.
GCSEs normally required: no formal qualification structure, but almost usually 5 GCSEs at grade C or above, to include English and maths.
GCSEs which may be useful: business studies/economics, modern languages, science, social sciences, statistics.
Other academic/training requirements: A-levels and often a degree.
Personality/physical requirements: Good communication skills (oral and written); clear, logical thought processes and analytical skills; strong interest in handling figures and interpreting statistics; ability to work to deadlines and under pressure.

PURCHASING/BUYING ASSISTANT

Entry levels: G+.
GCSEs normally required: Usually 4-5 GCSEs at grade C or above, including English and maths.
GCSEs which may be useful: Business studies/economics; IT.
Other academic/training requirements: None before entry.
Personality/physical requirements: Good organisational abilities and methodical approach; liking for clerical work; ability to handle figures.

PURCHASING OFFICER/BUYER

Entry levels: G+, GD, A, AD.
GCSEs normally required: Usually 4-5 GCSEs at grade C or above, to include English and maths.
GCSEs which may be useful: Business studies/economics, IT.
Other academic/training requirements: A-levels and/or a degree or business studies qualification.
Personality/physical requirements: Self confidence and willingness to take responsibility; good organisational abilities and communication skills; smart appearance; ability to get on with suppliers/manufacturers; willingness to travel and work unsocial hours; good business/financial sense.

RETAIL MANAGER

Entry levels: G+, GD, A, AD.
GCSEs normally required: Entry varies, but often a minimum of 4-5 GCSEs at grade C or above, preferably to include English and maths.
GCSEs which may be useful: Business studies/economics.
Other academic/training requirements: Some companies only recruit applicants with A-levels (or BTEC equivalent) or degrees (any subject).
Personality/physical requirements: Self confidence; good organisational abilities; ability to supervise staff; willingness to shoulder responsibility; good manner with customers; smart appearance; willingness to work long and unsocial hours and, often, to move for promotion.

SALES REPRESENTATIVE/MANAGER
Entry levels: G, G+.
GCSEs normally required: No formal requirements, but good general education is expected and some GCSEs at grade C or above are an advantage. Preferred subjects are English and maths.
GCSEs which may be useful: See above.
Other academic/training requirements: none necessarily before entry but A-levels, or even a degree, are required for technical sales work.
Personality/physical requirements: Self confidence; pleasant manner and smart appearance; ability to get on with people and to be persuasive when necessary; usually, ability to drive and minimum age 21.

SHOP ASSISTANT/SHELF FILLER/CASHIER
Entry levels: N, G.
GCSEs normally required: Usually no formal requirements, but applicants with some GCSEs at grade E or above, especially in English and maths, may be preferred.
GCSEs which may be useful: See above.
Other academic/training requirements: None before entry.
Personality/physical requirements: Pleasant manner and appearance; honesty; high standards of personal hygiene; reasonable numeracy; quick worker; willingness to do repetitive work; often, willingness to work at weekends and/or evenings.

TELEPHONE SALES CLERK
Entry levels: G, G+.
GCSEs normally required: No specific requirements, but applicants with a couple of higher grade GCSEs, especially in English and maths, may be preferred.
GCSEs which may be useful: See above.
Other academic/training requirements: None before entry.
Personality/physical requirements: good voice and telephone manner; ability to be persuasive without putting potential customers off; liking for clerical work and attention to detail; liking for sedentary job and, with some employers, willingness to work unsocial hours. Preference for applicants over 18.

See also – *I'M THINKING ABOUT A CAREER IN ART AND
DESIGN* for Display Dresser

I'M THINKING ABOUT A CAREER IN SCIENCE

BIOLOGIST/BIOCHEMIST
Entry levels: GD, A, AD.
GCSEs normally required: 5 GCSEs at grade C or above, to include
English, maths, science.
GCSEs which may be useful: Statistics.
Other academic/training requirements: Science A-levels or Advanced
GNVQ and usually a science degree.
Personality/physical requirements: Real scientific interests; attention
to accuracy and detail; usually, a liking for teamwork; often,
organisational and supervisory abilities.

ENVIRONMENTAL SCIENTIST/ECOLOGIST
Entry levels: AD.
GCSEs normally required: Good spread of GCSEs at grade C or
above, to include English, maths, science.
GCSEs which may be useful: Geography, geology.
Other academic/training requirements: Science/maths A-levels
preferred (sciences are not essential), then a degree.
Personality/physical requirements: Genuine interest in the
environment; good communication skills; analytical mind; liking
for teamwork and outdoor work.

GEOLOGIST/GEOPHYSICIST
Entry levels: AD.
GCSEs normally required: Good spread of GCSEs at grade C or
above, to include English, maths and science.
GCSEs which may be useful: Engineering/technology subjects;
geology; geography.
Other academic/training requirements: Science/maths A-levels, then a
degree.
Personality/physical requirements: Good judgment and ability to

accept responsibility; good communications skills and organisational ability; often, willingness to work abroad and/or travel; thoroughness.

INDUSTRIAL CHEMIST/FOOD SCIENTIST/PHARMACEUTICALS SCIENTIST

Entry levels: GD, A, AD.

GCSEs normally required: 5 GCSEs at grade C or above, to include English, maths and science.

GCSEs which may be useful: Modern languages.

Other academic/training requirements: Science A-levels or Advanced GNVQ, and very often a science degree.

Personality/physical requirements: Real scientific/ technologic interests; attention to accuracy and detail; good organisational and supervisory abilities; liking for teamwork.

INFORMATION SCIENTIST

Entry levels: AD.

GCSEs normally required: Good spread of GCSEs at grade C or above, to include English, maths, science and preferably modern languages.

GCSEs which may be useful: IT.

Other academic/training requirements: A-levels, then a degree.

Personality/physical requirements: Enquiring, research-oriented mind and liking for solving problems; excellent communication skills (written and oral); interest in information technology; ability to get on well with people. For scientific jobs, scientific interest and qualifications are needed.

LABORATORY TECHNICIAN

Entry levels: G+, GD, A.

GCSEs normally required: 4 GCSEs at grade C or above, to include maths and science.

GCSEs which may be useful: English, IT.

Other academic/training requirements: None before entry, although many entrants do have A-levels (or equivalent), some a Higher National Diploma.

Personality/physical requirements: Accuracy and attention to detail and accuracy; ability to follow precise instructions and record information clearly; ability to use technical equipment.

MATHEMATICIAN/STATISTICIAN

Entry levels: AD.
GCSEs normally required: Good spread of GCSEs at grade C or above, to include English and maths.
GCSEs which may be useful: Science; business studies/ economics; IT.
Other academic/training requirements: Maths A-level(s), then a degree.
Personality/physical requirements: Thoroughness and attention to detail; real mathematical ability; insight and innovation; clear thought processes and analytical ability; often, a liking for teamwork; communication skills.

METALLURGIST/MATERIALS SCIENTIST

Entry levels: AD.
GCSEs normally required: Good spread of GCSEs at grade C or above, to include English, maths, science.
GCSEs which may be useful: Engineering/technology subjects.
Other academic/training requirements: Science/maths A-levels, then a degree in metallurgy, materials science or other relevant subject.
Personality/physical requirements: Thoroughness and attention to detail; enquiring mind and analytical abilities; liking for teamwork.

METEOROLOGIST

Entry levels: AD.
GCSEs normally required: Good spread of GCSEs at grade C or above, to include maths, English and science.
GCSEs which may be useful: IT, astronomy.
Other academic/training requirements: Science/maths A-levels, then a degree (usually physics, maths or meteorology) or, sometimes, a BTEC/SKIVE higher national award.
Personality/physical requirements: Attention to detail; good observational abilities; good communication skills (oral and written); liking for teamwork; insight and analytical abilities.

PHYSICIST/ASTRONOMER/ASTROPHYSICIST

Entry levels: AD.
GCSEs normally required: Good spread of GCSEs at grade C or above, to include maths, English, science.
GCSEs which may be useful: Engineering/technology subjects,

astronomy, IT.

Other academic/training requirements: Science/maths A-levels, then a degree.

Personality/physical requirements: Strong mathematical and scientific interests and abilities; meticulous attention to accuracy and detail; thoroughness; creativity and innovative approach to solving problems.

TECHNICAL WRITER

Entry levels: AD.

GCSEs normally required: A good spread of GCSEs at grade C or above, to include English, maths, science.

GCSEs which may be useful: Design and technology, IT.

Other academic/training requirements: A-levels (or equivalent) and usually a degree or a higher national award in a science/engineering subject.

Personality/physical requirements: Excellent communication skills, especially written; great attention to detail; thoroughness; ability to work to deadlines and under pressure.

I'M THINKING ABOUT A CAREER IN CONSTRUCTION AND LAND SERVICES

ARCHITECT

Entry levels: AD.

GCSEs normally required: Good spread of GCSEs at grade C or above, to include English and maths or science, and preferably art.

GCSEs which may be useful: Design and technology, social sciences, IT.

Other academic/training requirements: A-levels (or equivalent), then a degree in architecture.

Personality/physical requirements: Ability in design and creativity; practical approach; interest in people and their behaviour; good communication skills.

ARCHITECTURAL/SURVEYING TECHNICIAN

Entry levels: G+, GD, A, AD.
GCSEs normally required: Usually 4-5 GCSEs at grade C or above, to include maths, English and science.
GCSEs which may be useful: Design and technology, IT.
Other academic/training requirements: Entry after GCSEs, A-levels or BTEC/SKIVE award courses.
Personality/physical requirements: Drawing ability; meticulous and careful worker; ability to work in a team; technical understanding.

BRICKLAYER/CARPENTER/PLUMBER/ PLASTERER

Entry levels: G.
GCSEs normally required: Qualifications not essential but a general standard of GCSEs at grade E or above will help. Maths, science, design and technology may be preferred.
GCSEs which may be useful: Practical/craft subjects.
Other academic/training requirements: Apprenticeship/Youth Training to get started.
Personality/physical requirements: Fitness; reasonable strength; ability to work in a team; care and thoroughness; for some jobs, ability to read drawings; common sense and safety consciousness; good practical skills.

BUILDER'S LABOURER

Entry levels: N, G.
GCSEs normally required: No specific requirements.
GCSEs which may be useful: Practical/craft subjects.
Other academic/training requirements: None before entry.
Personality/physical requirements: Minimum age usually 18. Fitness and lots of energy; strength; common sense and safety consciousness; ability to put up with weather conditions.

BUILDING SURVEYOR/BUILDING CONTROL OFFICER

Entry levels: G+, GD, AD.
GCSEs normally required: 5 GCSEs at grade C or above, to include maths and English.
GCSEs which may be useful: Design and technology.

Other academic/training requirements: Entry either after GCSEs and BTEC/SKIVE National Diploma, A-levels or Higher National Diploma/degree.
Personality/physical requirements: Practical approach; thoroughness and care; attention to detail; good communication skills; aptitude for problem solving; willingness to take on responsibilities.

BUILDING TECHNICIAN
Entry levels: G+,GD.
GCSEs normally required: 4 GCSEs at grade C or above, including English, maths, science.
GCSEs which may be useful: Design and technology, practical subjects.
Other academic/training requirements: None before entry, though you could take a course such as BTEC/SKIVE National Diploma.
Personality/physical requirements: Practical abilities; organisational/supervisory abilities; liking for teamwork.

BUILDING TECHNOLOGIST/SITE MANAGER
Entry levels: AD.
GCSEs normally required: 4-5 GCSEs at grade C or above, to include English, maths and science.
GCSEs which may be useful: Design and technology.
Other academic/training requirements: A-levels (preferably science), then Higher National Diploma or degree in building.
Personality/physical requirements: Practical approach to problems; good planning and organisational abilities; willingness to accept responsibilities; supervisory skills and ability to get on with all types of people.

CARTOGRAPHER
Entry levels: AD.
GCSEs normally required: Good spread of GCSEs at grade C or above, to include English, maths.
GCSEs which may be useful: Geography, science, art/design, IT.
Other academic/training requirements: Higher National Diploma or degree after A-levels (geography or maths preferred).
Personality/physical requirements: Careful attention to detail; precision; patience; interest in using computers.

CARTOGRAPHIC DRAUGHTSMAN/WOMAN

Entry levels: G+,GD,A.

GCSEs normally required: 2-3 GCSEs at grade C or above, to include subjects from: English, maths, geography, art, design and technology, science, languages.

GCSEs which may be useful: IT.

Other academic/training requirements: Entry possible after GCSEs, A-levels or BTEC/SKIVE National Diploma.

Personality/physical requirements: Meticulous concern for accuracy and precision; patience; design and drawing ability; interest in using computers; normal colour vision.

ELECTRICIAN

Entry levels: G,G+.

GCSEs normally required: Good general education, preferably with GCSEs (perhaps grade C or above) in English, maths, science.

GCSEs which may be useful: Design and technology, practical/craft subjects.

Other academic/training requirements: Youth Training/apprenticeship.

Personality/physical requirements: Ability to concentrate on detail; normal colour vision; manual dexterity; safety consciousness.

GLAZIER/ROOFER/TILER/SCAFFOLDER

Entry levels: N,G.

GCSEs normally required: No specific requirements, but some GCSEs may be a help.

GCSEs which may be useful: Maths, science, craft/practical subjects.

Other academic/training requirements: Perhaps an apprenticeship or Youth Training scheme.

Personality/physical requirements: Fitness and energy; usually, ability to stand working at heights; liking for working in a team; practical abilities; common sense and safety consciousness.

PAINTER AND DECORATOR

Entry levels: N, G.

GCSEs normally required: No special requirements, but some GCSEs at grade E or above may be preferred, especially maths.

GCSEs which may be useful: Practical/craft/art subjects.

Other academic/training requirements: Youth Training/apprenticeship.

Personality/physical requirements: careful and tidy worker; good hand skills; thoroughness; good eye for colour and normal colour vision; reasonable fitness; ability to climb ladders and work at height.

SURVEYOR

Entry levels: G+, GD, A, AD.
GCSEs normally required: 5 GCSEs at grade C or above, to include English and preferably science.
GCSEs which may be useful: Geography, geology, design and technology.
Other academic/training requirements: Entry possible after GCSEs, A-levels and very often Higher National Diploma or degree.
Personality/physical requirements: Reasonable fitness; draughting skills for some branches; attention to detail; smart appearance and good interpersonal skills for some branches.

TOWN PLANNER

Entry levels: AD.
GCSEs normally required: Good spread of GCSEs at grade C or above, to include English and maths, plus 1 of: history, geography, a modern language.
GCSEs which may be useful: Science, statistics, social sciences.
Other academic/training requirements: A-levels (or equivalent), then a degree.
Personality/physical requirements: Good communication skills (written and oral); ability to analyse information; liking for teamwork; good organisational abilities.

TOWN PLANNING TECHNICIAN

Entry levels: G+.
GCSEs normally required: 4 GCSEs at grade C or above, to include English (or subject testing use of written English) and maths.
GCSEs which may be useful: Geography, history, design and technology, economics, science.
Other academic/training requirements: None before entry, although some entrants have BTEC/SKIVE awards.
Personality/physical requirements: Liking for teamwork; thoroughness and attention to detail.

See also – *I'M THINKING ABOUT A CAREER IN SELLING, MARKETING OR ADVERTISING* for Estate Manager

See also – *I'M THINKING ABOUT A CAREER IN 'THE GREAT OUTDOORS'* for Landscape Architect

I'M THINKING ABOUT A CAREER IN MANUFACTURING INDUSTRY

BAKER
Entry levels: N, G, G+, GD.
GCSEs normally required: No set requirements, but GCSEs, especially in English, maths and science, may enable you to take a course in baking.
GCSEs which may be useful: Science, maths, home economics.
Other academic/training requirements: BTEC National Diploma course available as one entry route.
Personality/physical requirements: High standards of hygiene; strength and fitness; ability to stand high temperatures; willingness to work unsocial hours.

FACTORY WORKER (Skilled)
Entry levels: G.
GCSEs normally required: Perhaps 2-3 GCSEs at grade E or above. Preferred subjects may be maths, science, design and technology/practical subjects.
GCSEs which may be useful: See above.
Other academic/training requirements: None before entry.
Personality/physical requirements: Ability to cope with repetitive work; ability in teamwork; safety consciousness and common sense; practical skills.

FACTORY WORKER (Unskilled or Semi-skilled)
Entry levels: N, G.
GCSEs normally required: No special requirements.
GCSEs which may be useful: Practical/craft subjects.
Other academic/training requirements: None before entry.

Personality/physical requirements: Some jobs have minimum age limit of 18. Patience and ability to cope with repetitive work; good with hands; safety consciousness.

FOUNDRY WORKER
Entry levels: N.
GCSEs normally required: No set requirements.
GCSEs which may be useful: Practical/craft subjects; design and technology.
Other academic/training requirements: None before entry.
Personality/physical requirements: Fitness and strength; ability to withstand very high temperatures; practical abilities and safety consciousness.

INDUSTRIAL TECHNICIAN (eg Polymers, Brewing, Textiles, Photographic Processing)
Entry levels: G+.
GCSEs normally required: Ranging from no formal qualifications to 4-5 GCSEs at grade C or above, usually including maths and science, with English preferred.
GCSEs which may be useful: Design and technology/engineering, practical subjects, IT.
Other academic/training requirements: None before entry. BTEC National route available for those with 4 GCSEs.
Personality/physical requirements: Practical approach; ability with machinery and technical equipment; supervisory and organisational abilities; liking for teamwork.

INDUSTRIAL TECHNOLOGIST (eg Printing, Textiles, Food, Packaging)
Entry levels: AD.
GCSEs normally required: Good spread of GCSEs at grade C or above, to include maths, science and usually English.
GCSEs which may be useful: See above.
Other academic/training requirements: A-levels (sciences/maths), then a Higher National Diploma or degree.
Personality/physical requirements: Strong technical/ scientific interests and abilities; practical approach; good organisational abilities; business sense.

PACKER

Entry levels: N, G.
GCSEs normally required: No formal requirements.
GCSEs which may be useful: Practical subjects.
Other academic/training requirements: None before entry.
Personality/physical requirements: Practical skills – good with hands; ability to put up with routine, repetitive work; quick and tidy worker.

PRINTING WORKER

Entry levels: G, G+.
GCSEs normally required: GCSEs at grade E or above are likely to be preferred, especially in English, maths, science.
GCSEs which may be useful: Art, design and technology.
Other academic/training requirements: None before entry.
Personality/physical requirements: Dexterity and practical skills; care and accuracy; normal colour vision; liking for using machinery.

PRODUCTION MANAGER

Entry levels: A, AD.
GCSEs normally required: 4-5 GCSEs at grade C or above, usually including English, maths and science.
GCSEs which may be useful: Engineering/design and technology, IT, business studies/economics.
Other academic/training requirements: A-levels and degree (preference for science/engineering/business subjects).
Personality/physical requirements: Organisational and management abilities; sound business sense; practical approach to problems; diplomacy and interpersonal skills; drive and energy.

SEWING MACHINIST/MILLINER

Entry levels: N, G.
GCSEs normally required: None in particular.
GCSEs which may be useful: Home economics (dress and fabrics).
Other academic/training requirements: None before entry.
Personality/physical requirements: Neat and careful worker; ability to work quickly; no objection to repetitive and sedentary work.

WOODWORKING MACHINIST/FURNITURE MAKER

Entry levels: N, G.

GCSEs normally required: Good general education preferred, with GCSEs in maths and design and technology.

GCSEs which may be useful: Practical/craft subjects.

Other academic/training requirements: None before entry, but BTEC and degree routes available for those with necessary qualifications..

Personality/physical requirements: Attention to detail and care in using machinery; practical skills; ability to put up with repetitive work.

See also – *I'M THINKING ABOUT A CAREER IN ENGINEERING & I'M THINKING ABOUT A CAREER IN SCIENCE*

Please refer to the appendix at the back of this book for an alphabetical index of careers listed in this section.

---

9. HOW HAS GCSE WORKED IN PRACTICE?

HOW DO GCSE RESULTS COMPARE WITH THE OLD SYSTEM?

Generally, very favourably. The overall pattern is one of higher standards, although the Government's expressed reservations about some aspects of the examination and its assessment procedures has led to some of the changes described in this book.

31.3% of Year 11 candidates in the UK obtained 5 or more A-C grades in 1990. This had risen to 36.7% by 1993.

HOW WILL I GET MY RESULTS?

Each Examining Group is responsible for publishing the results of its examinations on a jointly agreed date, usually towards the end of August.

The results will be sent to your school or college who will then forward them to you. Some schools and colleges make arrangements for candidates to collect their results in person (often later on the day of their arrival). Your school or college will always tell you the date you can expect to receive or collect them.

HOW CAN I BE SURE THAT MY GRADE WILL BE ACCURATE?

Proven inaccuracies have been very few in number, measured against the millions of subject entries. Remember that the system of checking marking and results includes impartial observers and that the checking system is very thorough.

There is an appeals system for GCSE grading. In the first instance, you appeal to your school or college and – if they think a mistake has been made – they will put in an appeal to the Examining

111

Group on your behalf: it costs about £15 for an exam script to be re-examined, but schools are reimbursed if they win their case. The Independent Appeals Authority for School Examinations only becomes involved when the exam boards' own procedures have been exhausted – and only hears a handful of appeals each year.

In Scotland, by contrast, anyone can query results, though not everyone can instigate the formal appeal.

But, before even considering the appeals process, remember that your teachers are in a good position to make an accurate assessment of your work. The likelihood of an error in the marking is very low.

HAS GCSE REALLY PROVED SUITABLE FOR ALL?

GCSE is open to anyone at school or college, whatever their ability. However, it is commonly held not to have been quite as successful for some less able students. This is because of the high requirement for literacy and the demands of coursework.

It is difficult to provide courses and exams that will suit the whole age group. GCSE does fall short of genuinely catering for all and attempts are still being made to come up with alternative courses and methods of assessment for the less able.

There is a range of courses currently available outside the GCSE, including the Youth Award scheme, RSA Initial Awards, the Certificates of the WJEC and Basic Tests from the RSA. Your school will be able to tell you whether it is operating any of these alternatives.

WHAT ADVICE CAN YOU GIVE ME ON WHICH LEVEL OF EXAM TO CHOOSE?

In subjects where there is a choice of level, you must first of all listen to the advice of your subject teachers. Try to avoid the temptation of ignoring what they say just because the alternative option holds out the possibility of a higher – or safer – grade. They are probably the best judges of your potential.

WHAT DIFFERENCE HAS GCSE MADE TO THE WAY MY SUBJECTS ARE TAUGHT?

Most importantly, it has raised standards of teaching. In the early years of GCSE, HMI visits to schools indicated a significant improvement in the standard of lessons observed.

In particular, the HMIs found that study for the new exam had both raised students' motivation and performance and teaching quality. They stated that 'teachers appear to have become more aware of what [students] are capable of achieving'.

GCSE has led to a marked improvement in oral and written work, and more and better practical and investigative work. It has increased the ability of students to show what they know, understand and can do, especially in their coursework. The additional emphasis given to positive achievement in both coursework and the exams is probably the greatest success of GCSE.

WILL GCSE PREPARE ME FOR STUDY AT HIGHER LEVEL?

The GCSE is more of a challenge than the old O-level. HMIs expressed the view that it is 'sufficient of a challenge to form a sound intellectual basis for students going on to A-level'. GCSE has already had a positive impact on the numbers of young people staying on in full-time education in order to take A-levels or equivalent courses.

A-levels themselves have begun to change and may need to be further revised, partly to reflect the differences in the GCSE syllabuses. In a more positive sense, they should also change in order to take maximum benefit from the new skills being measured by the GCSE.

Remember that you need to do REALLY WELL in a subject at GCSE to consider taking it at A-level. Even a C grade is not a good indicator for A-level success in some subjects. This does NOT preclude your taking on A-levels (or other higher-level courses) of which you have no previous experience, as long as this is not simply an 'escape route' and you do have some evidence of your ability to cope.

10. THE GCSE IN NORTHERN IRELAND

In Northern Ireland, the GCSE is administered by the Northern Ireland Council for the Curriculum, Examinations and Assessment (CCEA). The Council advises the Department of Education for Northern Ireland (DENI) on assessment and examinations generally. GCSE syllabuses and examinations in Northern Ireland comply with the GCSE general and subject criteria, taking into account where necessary the distinctive features of the Northern Ireland common curriculum.

WHAT GCSE SUBJECTS ARE AVAILABLE IN NORTHERN IRELAND?

Accounting
Additional Mathematics
Art and Design
Biology: Human
Business Studies
Classical Civilisation (Greek and Roman)
Computer Studies
Craft, Design and Technology (Design and Communication)
Craft, Design and Technology (Design and Realisation)
Drama
Economics
English
English Literature
French
Geography
German
Greek
History
Home Economics
Irish (Gaeilge)
Italian

Latin
Mathematics
Motor Vehicle and Road User Studies
Music
Personal and Social Education
Physical Education
Religious Studies
Science: Biology
Science: Chemistry
Science: Double Award (Modular and Non-Modular)
Science: Geology
Science: Physics
Science: Single Award (Modular and Non-Modular)
Social Science
Spanish
Technology (Product and Systems Design)
Textiles

As in England and Wales, new National Curriculum and GCSE requirements are currently being phased in, with interim arrangements operating from September 1994 until the new requirements take full effect in September 1996.

In Northern Ireland the Key Stage 4 (Years 11 and 12) curriculum consists of six Areas of Study, six educational (cross-curricular) themes and a course of religious education.

WHAT ARE THESE AREAS OF STUDY?

The six Areas of Study are:
English
Mathematics
Science and Technology
The Environment and Society
Creative and Expressive Studies (Physical Education)
Language Studies

Students who have taken GCSE in either English or Mathematics at the end of Year 11 do not have to follow the Key Stage 4 programme of study. However, they must take another cognate subject, eg English Literature (in the case of English) or Additional Mathematics or Statistics (in the case of Mathematics).

National Curriculum programmes of study are already operating in most Areas of Study: Physical Education comes into line in September 1995 and Environment and Society courses – including History, Geography, Business Studies and Home Economics – in September 1996. From September 1996 courses in compulsory subjects which do not have programmes of study will have to be approved by DENI on the advice of CCEA.

Further changes scheduled for the year 1996-1997 involve the two Areas of Study, The Environment and Society, and Language Studies.

In The Environment and Society, there will be a choice between:
a course from History/Geography/Business Studies/Home Economics
or
an approved course in Economics/Politics or modular provision selected from a range of modules to include Law in our Lives, Environmental Education, Information Technology, Health/Sex Education, Economic Awareness, Cultural Heritage, Careers Education.

From 1996, the Language Studies provision will consist of an approved course, eg GCSE or GNVQ unit(s) or GOML.

WILL I HAVE MUCH CHOICE?

Reduction in the statutory curriculum time (again from September 1996) is intended to allow schools further flexibility to meet pupils' needs. For example, this can be used to provide additional time for the compulsory subjects, to offer additional courses from within the Area of Study framework, or to provide additional elements such as Personal and Social Education and Careers Guidance.

WHAT ABOUT COURSEWORK?

Coursework weightings are also different in Northern Ireland. The maximum allocations for coursework are as follows:

Art and Design	60%
Biology: Human	24%
Business Studies	20%
CDT Design and Communication	45%
CDT Design and Realisation	50%
Classical Civilisation	20%
Economics	20%
English	40%
English Literature	30%
Geography	20%
History	30%
Mathematics	20%
Religious Studies	30%
Science: Biology	24%
Science: Chemistry	24%
Science: Double Award	28%
Science: Physics	24%
Science: Single Award	25%
Social Science	30%
Technology	45%

DO WE ALL SIT THE SAME EXAMS?

No. There are again tiering arrangements, but these are different in Northern Ireland.

The tiers of entry for Northern Ireland National Curriculum subjects are:

Mathematics	Tier P	grades D-G
	Tier Q	B-F
	Tier R	A*-D

Science	Tier P	D-G
(Double/Single)	Tier Q	B-D (B-E for Single Award)
	Tier R	A*-B
English	Tier S	C-G
	Tier T	A*-D

11. ... AND IN SCOTLAND

IS THE STRUCTURE OF THE SECONDARY CURRICULUM AND EXAMINATIONS THE SAME AS IN THE REST OF THE UK?

No. There are several major differences in the Scottish system. Firstly, pupils in Scotland begin their secondary schooling when they are about 12 years of age. The curriculum is divided into three stages, the first two of which are compulsory. In the first two years of secondary school (S1 and S2), pupils follow a broad and balanced educational programme. Towards the end of S2, they choose the courses they will study in S3 and S4.

DOES THIS MEAN THAT THERE IS MORE CHOICE FOR 14 AND 15 YEAR OLDS IN SCOTLAND?

Not entirely. In effect, Scotland has a national curriculum for this age group, since all schools are expected to follow certain guiding principles, as defined by the Scottish Consultative Council on the Curriculum (SCCC – the Scottish equivalent to the National Curriculum Council).

All pupils have to continue studying English, Mathematics, a modern European language and a Science course at S3 and S4. In addition, schools are asked to ensure that pupils select additional full or short courses meeting the requirements of eight "modes" or areas of study:

Language and Communication
Mathematical Studies and Applications
Scientific Studies and Applications
Social and Environmental Studies
Technological Activities and Applications
Creative and Aesthetic Activities
Physical Education
Religious and Moral Education

WHAT SORT OF SCHOOL-LEAVING EXAMINATIONS ARE THERE?

At the end of S4 the majority of pupils take examinations leading to the Scottish Certificate of Education (SCE). The courses taken lead to awards at Standard Grade and to short course awards, recorded on the Scottish Certificate of Education.

DO I HAVE TO TAKE EXAMS IN ALL THE DIFFERENT MODES?

Not as such. The S3 and S4 courses are meant to give each pupil adequate experience in all the modes, but the S Grade courses are not an exact match to the individual modes. A single course may contribute to several different modes.

Pupils may cover the entire mode requirement by choosing a Core course. For example, it is possible to meet the Technological Activities and Applications requirement by taking an S Grade course in Computing Studies, Craft & Design, Home Economics, Office and Information Studies or Technological Studies or relevant short courses or appropriate activities from these courses. It is also possible to meet this same mode requirement by taking other courses from a range of elective options.

ARE ALL THESE OPTIONS AVAILABLE IN ALL THE SCHOOLS?

No. Larger schools are normally able to offer a wider choice than smaller schools. National syllabuses also allow schools some flexibility in deciding on course content and on teaching and learning methods. So there may be differences in the teaching of a particular course between one school and another.

HOW MUCH TIME WILL I HAVE TO STUDY EACH SUBJECT?

There are recommended minimum and maximum time allocations for each pupil, based on the assumption that the syllabuses for English and Mathematics would need five 40-minute periods a week and those for other full courses four periods. The normal

121

minimum time requirement (in hours) for each of the modes, over the two-year period, is as follows:

Language and Communication	360
Mathematical Studies and Applications	200
Scientific Studies and Applications	160
Social and Environmental Studies	160
Technological Activities and Applications	80
Creative and Aesthetic Activities	80
Physical Education	80
Religious and Moral Education	80

The total of 1200 hours allocated to this core of the eight modes represents approximately 70% of the time available to pupils throughout S3 and S4.

WHAT HAPPENS FOR THE REST OF THE TIME?

In the remaining 30% of available class time, schools are able to offer a variety of short or modular courses of varying lengths. The most common format for such courses is that of modules leading to the award of the National Certificate by the Scottish Vocational Educational Council (SCOTVEC). The SCOTVEC modules include a number of courses that serve to complement the curriculum at S3 and S4.

The Scottish Examination Board (SEB) also provides a limited range of short courses which are certificated on the SCE. The courses offered are:

Classical Studies
Creative and Aesthetic Studies
Electronics
European Studies
Geology
Graphic Communication
Health Studies,
Nautical Studies
Religious & Moral Education
Statistics
Technological Studies

Schools can also offer short courses of their own design, which do not lead to national certification.

ARE STANDARD GRADE COURSES AND EXAMS THE SAME FOR ALL?

Not in all cases. In some areas, such as Mathematics, pupils follow courses at three levels, ie to suit different levels of ability. In other areas, such as English, the course is the same for all, but the skills to be acquired are differentiated to suit the different ability groups.

WHAT IS THE GRADING SYSTEM FOR THE STANDARD GRADE EXAMS?

For most courses, there are three separate examination papers at the end of the 2 years. They are set for Credit, General and Foundation levels.

Credit papers lead to awards at grade 1 or 2, General papers to awards at grade 3 or 4 and Foundation papers to awards at grade 5 or 6. A grade 7 is also available for those who complete the course but provide no evidence of significant attainment on it.

Normally, pupils take examinations covering two pairs of grades, either grades 1-4 or grades 3-6. This is intended to ensure that all pupils have the best opportunity to gain an award which reflects their real ability and achievement.

WHAT ELSE DO I NEED TO KNOW ABOUT THE ASSESSMENT SYSTEM?

It is essentially a performance or criteria related method of assessment. In other words, the award is based on the achievements of the individual pupil, measured against stated standards, rather than on how that individual's achievement compares with that of other candidates.

In order to achieve a particular grade within a particular level, candidates have to give evidence of achievement in all the basic aspects or 'elements' of the subject. For example, in English, candidates will receive separate assessments for Reading, Writing and Talking as well as an overall grade. A 'profile' of performance stating the grade obtained in each element then appears on the Certificate beside the overall award for the course.

HOW WILL THESE ELEMENTS BE ASSESSED?

In a variety of different ways. In most courses, candidates will have to demonstrate attainment in oral or practical skills and these skills will usually be assessed internally by the class teacher on the basis of work done during the course.

Other elements, such as Writing in English will be assessed on the basis of a folio submitted to the SEB, together with a written examination. Others will be assessed through a written examination alone.

In all cases, even where an element is assessed externally, teachers will have submitted estimated grades to the Board. These can be used to improve the Board's grades in the case of any disagreement.

If an assessment is not available for any element, for whatever reason, no overall grade can be given for the course. The only exception to this is when a candidate is not able to offer an element because of a particular handicap or impairment.

WHAT ABOUT THE ASSESSMENT OF SHORT COURSES?

The individual school is responsible for assessing candidates taking short courses, with the SEB moderating school assessments to ensure national standards.

The SCE then records any SEB short courses which have been completed successfully.

WHAT HAPPENS AT 16+?

There is a further, optional stage of 1 to 2 years for pupils aged 16 to 18 who wish to stay on at school. At present, over 75% of S4 pupils are returning to school for S5.

The range of courses available includes courses leading to the Higher Grade of the SCE and to the Certificate of Sixth Year Studies.

Pupils who achieve a Credit Level award at Standard grade will normally sit the Higher examination in that subject after just one more year of study, ie at about age 17. Pupils who achieve General will probably require a further two years of study, but it should be noted that not all schools can offer a Higher Grade course spread over a two-year period.

Higher Grades have been going through a period of revision, but this has not affected their place in the Scottish educational system and they continue to provide the route for a significant proportion of students aiming to enter the professions, go to university or into other forms of higher education.

WHAT OTHER COURSES ARE AVAILABLE?

Although it is again subject to some changes, the Certificate of Sixth Year Studies (CSYS) remains available for students who obtain a pass at H grade in their fifth year and wish to continue their studies into a sixth year.

National Certificate modules are also available for students in S5 and S6 as an alternative or complement to Highers and CSYS.

The SEB is developing further short courses which will often be suitable for study in S5 and S6.

HIGHER STILL

A new system of post-16 education for all students is proposed for 1997-98. The aim of the 'Higher Still' Development Programme is to bring together Higher Grade courses, CSYS courses, SEB short courses, National Certificate modules, General Scottish Vocational Qualifications (GSVQs) and the National Certificate group awards into a single, coherent post-16 system.

Further details of the Higher Still Programme will be announced over the remainder of the development period, but pupils and parents can be assured that every effort is being made to ensure a smooth transition into the new system.

Pupils who are in S2 in session 1994/95 will be the new S5 – the first Higher Still candidates – in 1997/98 and progression routes from Standard Grades to Highers will continue to be available for these pupils.

12. LIFE AFTER GCSE – OPTIONS AT 16

MY OPTIONS AT 16 – HOW WILL THEY AFFECT MY CHOICE OF GCSES?

In another two years' you will be facing another decision – one that will shape your future. And the choice will be even greater, but, by the options you are making in your selection of GCSE subjects you are laying the foundation of that choice now.

So, before you make your final selection of GCSEs, think carefully about what you might decide to do later on.

The options at 16 are very wide indeed, but these are the major ones:

GETTING A JOB

There's no denying that for some school is just a chore – they can't wait to get out and earn their own living. However, fewer employers are now recruiting at 16. Of those that are, you should certainly be looking more seriously at those who are offering further training, preferably leading to a National Vocational Qualification. You need to think about what GCSEs would be preferred, or required, to start a job at 16.

GOING ON A TRAINING COURSE

You may decide not to stay at school. There are various training options for 16 year-olds. They include:

YOUTH TRAINING

Job opportunities at 16 are no longer easy to find. Youth Training is a halfway house between work and study. It gives you work experience, training and at least the minimum weekly training allowance. There's no guarantee of a job at the end, but very often it does result in one. And even if you don't land a permanent job, you would have some good experience to offer another employer. But how does all this affect GCSE decisions? Some Youth Training schemes have GCSE entry qualifications, so you should check that the GCSEs you choose are acceptable for any Youth Training option you may be considering.

The Youth Credits system (sometimes known by another name, such as Training Credits) allows.school and college leavers to choose and buy their own career training. It also entitles you to more careers advice and guidance to help you make the most of the opportunities available. It is available to every 16- and 17- year old leaving school or college in England after April 1995 and in Wales after April 1996.

MODERN APPRENTICESHIPS

This is the newest approach to training for young people: the first Modern Apprenticeships started in September 1994. Modern Apprenticeships are geared to individual needs and provide training to at least NVQ Level 3 (equivalent to 2 A levels).

VOCATIONAL COURSES

Other examination courses you can take include:

BTEC	Certificate/Diploma qualifications at First, National and Higher National Level. Some of the former BTEC First and National awards are being phased out and replaced by GNVQs.
City & Guilds	Examinations leading to skilled craft qualifications.
RSA	Royal Society of Arts examinations, principally covering the range of business and commercial studies.
LCCI	The London Chamber of Commerce and Industry, which offers examinations for office skills and secretarial studies.

STAYING ON AT SCHOOL

This will often involve taking A-levels or an Advanced GNVQ. Courses at this level are essential if you want to go on to take a degree.

A GNVQ Advanced qualification is broadly equivalent to a couple of A-Levels and entry onto such courses is therefore at a similar level to that for A-levels – with most schools and colleges asking for a minimum of four or five GCSEs at grade C or above, or equivalent qualifications. GNVQ Advanced Level qualifications meet the general requirements for entry to many degree courses. Successful students are also well placed to apply for a range of jobs with good prospects.

Post-16, the vocational areas currently or soon to be available at Advanced (and the other two GNVQ Levels) include:

- Art & Design
- Built Environment
- Business
- Distribution
- Engineering
- Health & Social Care
- Hospitality & Catering
- Information Technology
- Land Based Industries
- Leisure & Tourism
- Management
- Manufacturing
- Media & Communication
- Science

If taking A-levels, you'll probably opt for two or three subjects. The subjects you have taken at GCSE are bound to influence your choice of A-levels. A-levels are of a high standard and in some subjects it may not be easy to cope with the A-level syllabus unless you have studied the subject on a GCSE course – Languages and Sciences are examples of this. So, ask yourself which A-levels you might want to do before choosing your GCSEs.

Some of the subjects offered at A-level include the learning of specific practical skills. In some schools and colleges you can study Dance, Art or Sports Studies at A-level. And, if you want more variety in your studies, there is also the option of AS levels.

The AS level is there to help broaden your course of study. These courses reach the same high standard as A levels, but cover less ground. (Two AS levels are generally seen to be the equivalent of one A-level). If you are thinking about taking AS levels, consider which GCSEs would be appropriate to give you a good grounding in the subjects you would like to study.

OTHER OPTIONS IN THE SIXTH FORM OR AT COLLEGE

Many schools and colleges offer Foundation or Intermediate Level GNVQ courses for students in Year 12 onwards.

For GNVQ Intermediate courses, students are normally expected to have achieved something like 4 GCSEs at grades D-G or a Foundation GNVQ (or an NVQ at Level 1).

Entry onto GNVQ Foundation Level courses does not require any formal qualifications, although applicants need to show the ability to benefit from the course.

You may find that you are also able to take GCSEs in the sixth form. These are usually two-year courses, but sometimes there is the option of special one-year courses, especially in new subject areas. Coursework will still normally be a feature of these courses, but the syllabus will be designed to ensure you can carry it out within one year.

13. MAKING THE CHOICE

The National Curriculum has already greatly limited the number of options open to students in Years 10 and 11 (Years 11 and 12 in Northern Ireland). However, if your school continues to operate a system with any element of choice in the subjects to be taken at GCSE, it is important that you should think carefully about your choice. This book should have helped you get all the facts you need. You should now be ready to make your final choice.

Use this checklist to make your selection.

- make a list of all subjects your school is offering.

- tick subjects that are essential for your career.

- tick all the subjects your school insists that you take.

- tick any subjects you enjoy – are good at – want to take.

- tick any of the new subjects being offered that you would like to try or think would be useful.

- check to see if you have at least one subject from each of the major subject groups, ie:
  English
  Maths
  Modern Foreign Languages
  Sciences
  Humanities
  Creative Subjects (including Technology) and make sure you have taken advice before leaving out any one group.

- count up the number of subjects you have ticked. If it comes to more than six, check with your teachers how many subjects they think you can cope with.

- check the coursework commitment in each subject with your teachers.

- if there are too many subjects or the coursework commitment is too high, work through this list again, being more selective.

NOW, HOW DOES IT LOOK?

Horrendous?
Horrifying?
Difficult?
Look through the checklist again and be even more selective.

OR

Hard work?
Interesting?
OK?
Just right?
GO FOR IT!

BUT WHAT IF I DO CHOOSE THE WRONG SUBJECTS, WHAT CAN I DO?

Don't panic! It happens all the time.

It could be that you will suddenly get a new career idea and will realise you need to be studying something else. If you have chosen wisely in the first place, it is unlikely that many of the subjects you have opted for will be wrong. So, if you are part way through your GCSEs, the answer is to keep on studying and get the best possible grades you can in the subjects you are taking. That will always stand you in good stead. Who knows, you might change your mind yet again.

Then, when you get to the sixth form or move on to a college, you can take the extra subjects you need and, because you will be that much older, you should be able to take them in one year instead of the normal two – that is one of the advantages of the GCSE system.

MY GCSE DECISIONS

	SUBJECT GROUPS				
English	Maths	Sciences	Humanities	Creative subjects	Modern languages
1					
2					
3					

Appendix

Alphabetical Careers Index to Chapter 8 - pages 41-110

Other essential books from Trotman's...

The Complete Degree Course Offers 1996
by Brian Heap
26th Edition
This essential book for applicants to higher education includes points requirements for entry to all first degree courses, advice on how to choose a course and institution, information on how to complete the new section 10 on the UCAS form and much more.
Price: £15.50
Published April 1995

How To Choose Your Degree Course
by Brian Heap
4th Edition
The long awaited new edition of this book contains general advice on how to go about choosing which degree subject to study, looking at A-level subjects and their related courses, and at career groups and specific careers.
Price: £11.95
Published 1994

How To Choose Your Higher National Diploma Course
Second Edition
This extensively revised and updated publication provides information on: entrance requirements, course descriptions, selection criteria and procedures, intake numbers and applications received, sponsorship and work placements, employment statistics as well as information on GNVQs and NVQs.
Price: £14.95
Published 1993

Order Form (please photocopy)

Please send me the following books:

		Qty	Total
Degree Course Offers 1996	£15.50 + 2.50 p+p	_____	£_____
How To Choose Your Degree Course	£11.95 + 2.25 p+p	_____	£_____
How To Choose Your HND Course	£14.95 + 2.25 p+p	_____	£_____
		Total	**£_____**

Please call us on 081-332-2132 for Access and Visa orders and postage and packing rates for multiple copy orders.

Trotman books are available through good bookshops everywhere.

Cash Orders: Please make your cheque payable to **Trotman & Company** and send it to:
12 Hill Rise, Richmond, Surrey, TW10 6UA
Credit Orders: only for schools'/organisations' orders of **over £35**. Please attatch your **official order form** to ours. The original invoice will be sent with the books, payment is due within 28 days.